Adelheit von Rastenberg

Texts and Translations

Chair: Robert J. Rodini
Series editors: Jane K. Brown, Eugene C. Eoyang, Michael R. Katz,
Carol S. Maier, English Showalter, and Renée Waldinger

Texts

1. Isabelle de Charrière. *Lettres de Mistriss Henley publiées par son amie.* Ed. Joan Hinde Stewart and Philip Stewart. 1993.
2. Françoise de Graffigny. *Lettres d'une Péruvienne.* Introd. Joan DeJean and Nancy K. Miller. 1993.
3. Claire de Duras. *Ourika.* Ed. Joan DeJean. Introd. Joan DeJean and Margaret Waller. 1994.
4. Eleonore Thon. *Adelheit von Rastenberg.* Ed. and introd. Karin A. Wurst. 1996.

Translations

1. Isabelle de Charrière. *Letters of Mistress Henley Published by Her Friend.* Trans. Philip Stewart and Jean Vaché. 1993.
2. Françoise de Graffigny. *Letters from a Peruvian Woman.* Trans. David Kornacker. 1993.
3. Claire de Duras. *Ourika.* Trans. John Fowles. 1994.
4. Eleonore Thon. *Adelheit von Rastenberg.* Trans. George F. Peters. 1996.

ELEONORE THON

Adelheit von Rastenberg
An English Translation

Translated by
George F. Peters

Introduction by
Karin A. Wurst

The Modern Language Association of America
New York   1996

For information about obtaining permission to reprint material from
MLA book publications, send your request by mail (see address be-
low), e-mail (permissions@mla.org), or fax (212 533-0680).

Library of Congress Cataloging-in-Publication Data

Thon, Eleonore, 1753–1807.
    [Adelheit von Rastenberg. English]
    Adelheit von Rastenberg : an English translation / Eleonore
Thon ; translated by George F. Peters with an introduction by
Karin A. Wurst.
        p.   cm. — (Texts and translations. Translations ; 4)
    ISBN 0-87352-782-8 (paper)
    I. Peters, George F., 1944–   . II. Wurst, Karin A. III. Title.
IV. Series.
PT2534.T88A6513   1996
832' .6—dc20   96-31887
ISSN 1079-2538

Cover illustration: photograph of a sketch for a generic stage design
for chivalric plays, attributed to Domenico Quaglio. Untitled, un-
dated. Used with permission of the University of Cologne, Theater
Studies Collection.

Printed on recycled paper

Published by The Modern Language Association of America
10 Astor Place, New York, New York 10003-6981

TABLE OF CONTENTS

INTRODUCTION

We first meet Adelheit von Rastenberg in the solitude of the forest. The dialogue soon reveals the reason for her mysterious daily sojourns there. We understand that the forest serves as refuge from her domestic situation. Her arranged marriage is the source of her sadness. In their youth, Adelheit and the knight Adelbert von Hohenburg were in love with each other but were separated when Adelbert left for the Crusades. Her father then forced her to marry another suitor, Robert von Rastenberg. After several years, Adelbert returns to his beloved, hoping to rekindle their love. He wants her to flee with him and live as his common-law wife on his sister's estate. Adelheit and Adelbert's unexpected reunion in the forest plunges Adelheit into deep conflict: she is torn between her honor and duty on the one hand and her love for Adelbert on the other. The play dramatizes the negotiation of morality, ethics, and love.

As universal as they may seem, the concepts of love, duty, and desire change over time and differ from culture to culture. To understand the dilemma facing the heroine of Eleonore Thon's *Adelheit von Rastenberg*, we therefore need to examine the 1788 play in its social and literary contexts. The play raises questions about what constituted ethical behavior in late-eighteenth-century Germany; it also demonstrates that while literary works reflect their cultural context, they may in turn influence the formation and change of social value systems. In discussing the play, then, we need to ask the following questions: Who was Eleonore Thon, and how did her class and gender affect her drama and its reception? How was the play related to other plays of the period? Who made up the contemporary reading public, and how were its tastes formed? What has been the fate of *Adelheit von Rastenberg* in literary history?

Eleonore Thon née Röder or Rödern (born 27 Nov. 1753 in Eisenach, died 7 Apr. 1807 also in Eisenach) was the daughter of August Friedrich Röder, private secretary at the ducal court in Weimar. The family had lost its fortune and land during the Thirty Years' War and had relinquished the privileges of nobility. As upper-level civil servants at the court, the Röders occupied a social position between the nobility and the bourgeoisie. A comfortable and sophisticated lifestyle afforded Eleonore an excellent education near a court famous for its cultural life. She was fortunate in her godmother, Fräulein von Schlotheim; the former head governess to the princess of Saxe-Gotha provided Eleonore with an exceptionally solid education. According to the foremost nineteenth-century biographer of German-speaking women writers, Carl August Freiherr von Schindel, Eleonore received the best possible educational experience available to women. The focus was on the arts and letters; language and stylistics, music, and drawing occupied most of her time. Her talent as a writer was complemented by her determination and diligence. In 1782 Eleonore married Johann Karl Solomon Thon, who was to become privy councillor at the court in Weimar. She started to write before she married, but unlike many of her female contemporaries, she continued to find time for her literary pursuits during her marriage. Eleonore Thon had one son, Heinrich Christian Caspar. In 1796 she contracted an illness that in time paralyzed her completely. She died at fifty-four.

Eleonore Thon is the author of the widely read novel in three volumes *Julie von Hirtenthal: Eine Geschichte in Briefen* (1780–83; "Julie von Hirtenthal: A Story in Letters"), written in the tradition of Sophie La Roche's *Geschichte des Fräuleins von Sternheim* (1771; *The History of Lady Sophia Sternheim*), which in turn was inspired by Samuel Richardson. The moral quality of Richardson's novels *Pamela* and *Clarissa* attracted much attention and interest in Germany, and their popularity also enhanced the prestige of German prose fiction. Richardson's sentimental domestic novels focused on a female protagonist in the private sphere of family. With the new subject matter came a new theme: besieged womanhood. Female virtue facing male seduction and corruption is also at the heart of *Julie von Hirtenthal*. Like many novels by women, Thon's novel explores the psychological preconditions that make women susceptible to the advances of men. It suggests that women's vulnerability stems from a superficial lifestyle characterized by vanity and a lack of modesty. As a remedy for this deplorable situation, Thon and many others advocate the proper education of women. Thon's novel *Briefe von Karl Leuckford* (1782; "Letters from Karl Leuckford") follows the popular tradition of sentimental travel literature. The narrative is based on the fiction of a packet of letters found by chance.

It was with the tragedy *Adelheit von Rastenberg* (1788) that Thon found her voice in the genre of drama, although she did not abandon prose narratives. One year later her *Marianne von Terville: Eine Erzählung* (1798; "Marianne von Terville: A Tale") appeared. Both anonymously and under the pseudonym Jenny, she also published poems, translations, and essays in various important journals of the time, such as *Olla Potrida* (1788–90) and the famous Weimar journal, Friedrich Justin Bertuch's *Journal des Luxus und der Moden* (1786–90; "Journal of Luxury and Fashions").

Eleonore Thon belonged to the increasing number of women who took to writing in the last three decades of the eighteenth century. They participated in the life of the many smaller and larger cultural centers in the German states. In comparison with our selective and limited contemporary canon of eighteenth-century drama, a surprisingly large number of plays enlivened the quite diverse theaters in the various German cities (Kord). Moreover, a reading craze was sweeping the country and increasing the demand for literature. Women, especially of the upper middle class, responded enthusiastically to the cultural stimulation of literature, taking their place as both readers and authors in this arena. Reading habits changed dramatically; in addition to the traditional intensive form of reading religious texts, which was now also practiced with certain secular texts such as Johann Wolfgang Goethe's *Die Leiden des jungen Werthers* (1774; *The Sorrows of Young Werther*), extensive reading became customary. If the repeated reading of material had served to confirm social identity, literary variety challenged readers to reexamine and reconstruct their identities (Engelsing; Kittler; McCarthy). In this way, the increasing number of texts played an important role in the transformation of social and literary value systems. These changes were not welcomed in all circles. By the end of the century, authors and critics like Goethe would attribute the decline of literary standards to the influence of dilettante authors and readers, especially women.

In broad terms, women's increased literary production was linked to the German Enlightenment, which championed education and literacy. Replacing Latin as the learned language, the German vernacular facilitated the dissemination of knowledge. The intellectual climate created a larger pool of writers by encouraging those who had previously been excluded by a lack of formal education and training. The educated upper middle class considered writers to be an important resource for the negotiation of moral values. To the middle class, the bourgeoisie, literature became the central emancipatory force for "self-fashioning" (Greenblatt), that is, for the reinvention of the self. Situated between the private sphere of family and home and the public sphere of political institutions, the literary sphere fostered debate and discussions in newspapers, journals, and literature, as well as in secret societies (Freemasons).[1] Often, the literary changes anticipated and eased social change.

The transformation of the concept of familial love in the eighteenth century (Rosenberg; Wurst, *Familiale Liebe*) illustrates how literature anticipates and reinforces social change. Literature anticipated the intimate nuclear family long before it became a social reality. In a sense, literature contributed to the change from a household—where several generations and servants lived and worked together in an extended family unit—to an intimate or sentimental family group. The celebration of the sentimental family paradigm in German literature was influenced by models provided by Jean-Jacques Rousseau and, above all, Richardson. Domestic subject matter and female heroes, filling the pages of novels and occupying the stage, dominated the German literary imagination. Within the urban middle class, the gradual replacement of the household by the nuclear family was characterized by the separation of the spheres of production, domestic work, reproduction, and consumption. As compensated labor performed by men moved outside the home, the division of labor firmly ensconced in the home the functions performed and supervised by women. The celebration of the family as the ideal nucleus of the private sphere emphasized the importance of women as wives and mothers. At the core of these refashioned familial relationships was a changing concept of love. Love, as a form of communication and identity formation, occupied a key position in the literature of the eighteenth century.

At the same time, cultural sophistication became a status symbol for the bourgeoisie, adding another, noneconomic dimension to the growth of the middle class. Women were encouraged to take an active role in the intimate and aesthetic life of the home. It was in this role that they became important consumers of literature. Consequently, the century's significant and rapid increase in literary production in all genres was linked, in part, to literature's appeal to the female audience.

The abundance of new books brought new readers and writers into the cultural sphere. It also provoked an intense debate about the proper aesthetic qualities of literary products. If the critical discussion of high literature remained in the hands of the professionals, the diverse levels of literacy and literary-cultural competence were fragmenting the monolithic concept of literature. The number of casual readers with limited education increased, and their tastes and preferences began to drive the market. Almanacs, journals, and newspapers created a hunger for novelty; people were driven to read primarily by curiosity. Instead of critical, distancing, and reflective reading, uncritical consumption became the dominant mode of literary reception in the nonprofessional realm. These two modes of reading provoked different responses from critics and educators: on the one hand, encouragement to read and on the other, an express warning against so-called addictive reading. Both encouragement and warning were directed particularly at women, who were often singled out in discussions about literature, its formal and aesthetic qualities as well as its function and purpose. Of course, women were not the only new readers; lower-middle-class men, especially younger, nonprofessional men, also challenged traditional reading habits. Nevertheless, in the public debate, women were considered primarily responsible for the undesirable habit of uncritical reading. In a 1799 outline of a planned essay on dilettantism, Goethe and Friedrich Schiller, the icons of Weimar classicism, excluded women from the realm of "genuine art" and relegated them to the status of dilettantes, citing women's lack of educational preparation and professional status.

Because Weimar classicism was highly influential for canon formation in German literature, its assessment of women as dilettantes contributed significantly to a lack of interest in their works. During the nineteenth century,

Schiller and Goethe became the standard against which all other authors were measured. Whereas the new interest in philology and critical editions focused on canonized works, little editorial attention was given to those texts that fell short of the standard. Often such texts, not properly collected and preserved, slipped into obscurity. The invisibility of women's dramatic traditions is therefore a reflection less of eighteenth-century realities than of the reception history outlined above. There is some evidence that Eleonore Thon's play was in the contemporary canon around 1800. *Adelheit von Rastenberg* was one of a few plays by women included in a valuable listing of 225 bourgeois tragedies published between 1745 and 1798. Compiled by her contemporary, Christian Heinrich Schmid, a literary critic and professor of poetics at the University of Giessen, the listing invites several observations. The number of bourgeois tragedies was considerably larger than today's canon suggests (Gotthold Ephraim Lessing's *Miß Sara Sampson* [1755; *Miss Sara Sampson*] and *Emilia Galotti* [1772] and Schiller's *Kabale und Liebe* [1784; *Intrigue and Love*] are the plays of today's canon). Schmid's inclusion of several plays by women indicates that their plays, contrary to nineteenth-century literary historiography, were not automatically relegated to separate collections. The number of plays of knighthood or chivalric dramas increased in the 1790s; Thon's play is one of the twelve examples that Schmid puts in that category. The heyday of chivalric plays as a popular entertainment genre came in the nineteenth century. Today, they share the fate of obscurity with many popular plays of the past. Schmid, a scholar well versed in the theory and criticism of dramatic forms of his time, considered bourgeois tragedy the dominant genre and chivalric and historical drama subgenres.

Thon labeled *Adelheit von Rastenberg* a tragedy. Her preface adds that the story is based on an actual medieval German family chronicle. In fact, the play displays features not only of tragedy but also of bourgeois tragedy, and of chivalric and historical drama as well. It was both published separately and included in the first volume of the important collection *Deutsche Schaubühne* (1788; "German Theater"). Unfortunately, little is known about its performance history. On the basis of the author's social status, one may infer that the play was performed only in small private circles. However, Thon's inclusion in *Deutsche Schaubühne* and in some of the major biographical and bibliographical works of the time shows a high degree of contemporary reader interest in *Adelheit von Rastenberg*.

The patterns of the literary marketplace, outlined above, and the socialization of women in and for the private sphere inform Thon's literary production, with its focus on women as central characters. Not surprisingly, women of the bourgeoisie and the nobility had more in common with each other than their male counterparts did. Socialized primarily for life in the family, they tended to receive similar educational preparation, which in turn produced similar preferences and tastes in them as consumers of cultural products. Even women in the higher ranks of the German nobility were seen more in terms of their family context than as political figures or rulers (Becker-Cantarino). For women, class was a less distinguishing feature than gender was.

The relative unimportance of class distinctions for women might partially explain why Thon did not cast her play in the genre of bourgeois tragedy. One earmark of the genre is the issue of class conflict, often framed as conflict between vice and virtue. To avoid bourgeois tragedy's conventional class struggle, with its antagonistic ethical structure, she used the convention of the chivalric play. That the main characters are members of the nobility precludes an explicit class conflict; the play focuses, rather, on moral issues. But as the historian Reinhart Koselleck points out, morality is a political concept. In his *Kritik und Krise* (*Critique and Crisis*), he describes how the political system of absolutism was born from the conflicts of civil war. Absolutism created peace and stability by relegating individual opinions to the private sphere and at the same time consolidating all political powers and responsibilities in the public sphere. Under the protective umbrella of the private sphere, intellectuals theorized about creating a realm of morality and with it a system of self-regulation. They hoped that a self-regulatory ethics would eventually render the laws of the state obsolete. Their hope was grounded in the Enlightenment's philosophy of history, with its belief in calculability, planability, and progress. The ideal political state would be achieved when moral laws acquired a higher level of authority than political laws. In particular, the family was considered the realm of ideal human social interaction, where members were bound together by familial love and educated to become moral beings, as Jürgen Habermas argues in his *Strukturwandel der Öffentlichkeit* (*The Structural Transformation of the Public Sphere*).

The Enlightenment also fostered modes of self-regulation. The authority of theology and the old notion of familial alliances that have external codes of conduct

xvi

were increasingly replaced by internal principles of behavior. The philosophical and ethical thought of the time foregrounded the concept of virtue. Virtue was seen as the expression of an internal value system that governed relationships. Ideally, internal struggle resolved social conflict before it arose. Because this process required anticipating the views of others, it demanded a significant amount of reflection and a delay in decision making and action. The self-regulatory sense of morality provoked the criticism of a younger generation of intellectuals and authors, because it meant the repression of individual wishes and desires. With the writers of the Sturm und Drang, who voiced such concerns in the 1770s, the Enlightenment entered the stage of self-critique.

The German literary imagination was occupied not only by the conflict between personal morality and public politics but also by the concept of morality itself. In bourgeois tragedy, this conflict and this concept were negotiated in the setting of the domestic realm of the family. In this sense, bourgeois tragedy is ultimately also political. Thon's play, dealing with the negotiation of morality in the domestic realm, therefore fuses elements of bourgeois tragedy into chivalric drama. A brief comparison with the most famous chivalric drama, which was written fifteen years earlier, clarifies the uniqueness of Thon's play.

Goethe's *Götz von Berlichingen* (1773) represented a new prototype in the development of German drama. As part of a new historical awareness, each historical period began to be regarded in its own right; the medieval period, for example, lost its reputation as a barbaric dark age. At the same time, *Götz* created interest in the German national past. The protagonist, Götz, displays political qualities that the bourgeois class lacked in the eighteenth century: strength, self-confidence, and heroic spirit. He attacks the egoistic interests of particularism and its accompanying corruption. The conflict between Götz and his many antagonists takes place at the historical moment of transition between medieval and modern times. Selecting the period just before the establishment of absolutism was appropriate for two reasons: it set the stage not only for Götz's resistance to historical change but also for an eighteenth-century critique of the effects of that change. Goethe and his fellow Sturm und Drang authors considered Germany's fragmentation into many autocratically ruled principalities a major impediment to the development of a modern, economically strong, and politically influential middle class.

Adelheit von Rastenberg is not nationalistic and political in the way that *Götz* is. While *Götz* represents a change in value systems in the public sphere, *Adelheit* frames a similar change in the private sphere. Both plays show the individual faced with the challenge of self-realization in a value system in flux. Choosing a female protagonist makes a love interest the most realistic mode to portray the struggle of self-realization. The nationalistic element is relegated to the periphery. When Adelheit exclaims, "I am a German woman," the statement serves primarily as a characterization of personal conduct, signifying the highest ethical standards. It contrasts her sense of honor to that of Rastenberg's former lover, Franziska, a French woman who betrayed him.

Thon's play does not address the political dimension of nationhood or religious warfare. Instead, the influence of the genre of bourgeois tragedy underscores the private, interrelational, moral focus of the dramatic action. Despite Thon's explicit reference in the preface to the medieval period and the truthful historical core, the Crusade to Palestine is not important as a historical event. The Crusade is a device to set the domestic conflict in motion. The laws of war—coupled with familial authority—separate the lovers, Adelheit and Adelbert. The chivalric code compels Adelbert, a knight, to participate in the Crusade. In his absence, Adelheit's father forces her to marry a wealthier knight, Robert von Rastenberg. The focus is not the events of the public sphere, the male domain of battle in exotic lands, but the effects those events have on the private sphere at home.

Goethe's play was the model for several increasingly conservative chivalric dramas, which enjoyed success because of their exotic locales, costumes, and opportunities for special effects on the stage. Hinting at a return to an idealized past, these dramas allowed for the venting of discomfort and discontent with present conditions. On the whole, *Adelheit von Rastenberg* does not belong to this tradition. Thon uses neither an exotic locale nor special effects. The past is hardly idealized. Both time and place are strangely external to the plot and negotiated value system of this play. The text shows little interest in the historical specificity of medieval chivalric codes. Instead, it focuses on rights, duties, and responsibilities, that is, on the idea of morality in the author's own time. This lack of interest in historicity is one feature the play has in common with the popular dramas of knighthood. The problematic relation between love and family alliance is a decidedly eighteenth-century, not a medieval, conflict. After all, during the medieval period the highly cultured code of courtly love never questioned the primacy of the familial alliance. But a medieval setting allows dramatists to avoid the issue of class conflict so dominant in bourgeois tragedy.

All the main characters of Thon's play are engaged in negotiating morality, their autonomy, and the organization of power. The action contrasts competing and conflicting views of self-determination. To this end, love—the central force in women's socialization in the eighteenth century—is selected as the arena of conflict. During her arranged, loveless marriage to Robert von Rastenberg, Adelheit is unable to forget her true love, Adelbert von Hohenburg. His unexpected return and his suggestion that Adelheit flee with him present her with a deep moral dilemma: she is torn between her love for him and her honor and duty as wife. She decides against a life with Adelbert, but an intrigue forces her into an unintended nocturnal meeting with him. Adelheit's lack of faith in her husband renders her vulnerable. She distrusts her husband to such a degree that she considers him capable of having her poisoned in his absence. Furthermore, she is not portrayed heroically; she is, in her own words, "no heroine" and does not want to face a martyr's death. This combined lack of faith and heroism could be labeled her tragic flaw. Although in her heart she senses that Robert did not plan the murderous plot (later in the play, when she is stabbed, she suddenly knows that he is not the culprit), she wavers and eventually flees. Her nocturnal flight plays into the hands of her antagonist, Bertha, who is in love with Adelbert and who feels that Adelheit stands in her way to win his love. Bertha's obsessive desire for Adelbert, who has rejected her twice, turns into hatred. By fleeing, Adelheit presents Bertha with the opportunity to kill her.

As in many other literary texts of the time, a change in value systems fuels the dramatic conflict. In *Adelheit von Rastenberg*, the changing role of the family—the transition from extended household to nuclear family—creates instability. A sanctioned marriage between socially and economically equal parties, a marriage governed by family duty and not erotic love, is beginning to give way to a more volatile, sentimental love.[2]

Thon's drama foregrounds the precarious position of the individual in modern intimate relationships. Lacking the stabilizing tradition of family alliances, they provide a certain amount of freedom but also create a sense of insecurity. The medieval setting gives the dramatist the opportunity to experiment with an ahistorical clash of mutually exclusive stages in the development of the love paradigm. It allows her to reintroduce the family alliance as part of her unique representation of the problems inherent in the sentimental love paradigm. Sexuality plays an intrinsic but not necessarily positive role—at least not for Thon's women characters. Her presentation of sexuality is ambivalent. Her concept of love is more the sentimental paradigm than an anticipation of romantic love. But just as her sentimental paradigm is contaminated by sexual tensions, the alliance system is contaminated by the desire to sentimentalize and eroticize the family, which makes marriage much more than a means for the transmission of wealth and name.

Adelheit's fate displays two paradigms of social integration. Initially, she must follow her father's wishes and put family alliance above her desires, above her sentimental love for Adelbert. Action and imagery emphasize the violence done to her by her father and by her intended husband. As the helpless victim, she is literally dragged to the altar. Robert von Rastenberg ignores her pleas for mercy. His explanation is that he himself is in the throes of passion and thus is not master of his destiny; he insists on marrying her. Robert's position as her father's designated successor allows him to conflate love and desire with family alliance. With the wedding, the rights of the father transfer to the husband; Adelheit honors and respects her husband's public authority and fulfills her duties in the household, but she refuses a private, intimate relationship, thus separating the two paradigms of family that Robert wants to merge. Because the match is not based on reciprocity, she withholds sentimental love. Her hand belongs to Robert, but her heart still belongs to Adelbert.

On his return from the Crusades, Adelbert von Hohenburg hopes to resume his relationship with Adelheit. He justifies his dishonorable request with the argument that the sentimental lovers have a prior right and that Rastenberg is a villain who took Adelheit from him. Adelbert therefore does not consider their clandestine flight morally reprehensible. His insistence on the supremacy of sentimental love is an integral part of his desire for autonomy. His request, however, destabilizes the social status quo and causes a power struggle.

The realm most closely associated with Adelheit is not the home, the intimacy of domestic living, but the seclusion of the forest. The forest affords her the individualistic but limited space where she deems herself free from her duties as wife and stepmother. The division of theatrical space into home and forest creates meaning; it portrays Adelheit's divided self. But both home and forest are multivalent. As the natural realm of the forest signifies not only freedom but also danger, the cultural realm of the home signifies not only safety but also oppression. When Rastenberg's suspicions against Adelheit mount, her home turns literally into a prison, as the metaphor of the tower, bastion of patriarchal might, suggests.

With Adelbert's return, the precarious balance between Adelheit's honor and family alliance and her desire for self-fulfillment, which she initially considered embodied in her love for Adelbert, is disturbed anew. This time, however, she has a choice and must make a decision. Her panic on seeing Adelbert and hearing his demands prompts her to rush home to her confidante, Elisabeth. Her flight resembles the famous scene in Lessing's *Emilia Galotti*— when Emilia flees from the church into the arms of her mother to escape the seduction of the prince on the day of her wedding to Count Appiani. *Emilia Galotti* is constructed around a lucky coincidence that enables the family alliance system to coexist with the sentimental love paradigm. Count Appiani, the beloved future son-in-law, is not only the worthy and fully sanctioned successor to Emilia's father but also the ideal sentimental lover. Emilia's anxiety is caused by her intuition that this new paradigm, which equates sentimental familial love with love between the couple, ignores and devalues the force of sensuality and sexuality.

Adelheit's turmoil in the analogous scene is given no explanation beyond the comment that the meeting with her "soul mate" does not provide Adelheit with the calming sense of closure that she had wished for. The structure of the play precludes such an explanation. Should we read this allusion to *Emilia Galotti* as a metonymic replacement for the unspeakable, that is, a woman's desire? Adelbert is a much more physical lover than Count Appiani; he can hardly keep his hands off Adelheit, and she virtually has to pull away from his embrace. Combining the traits of Count Appiani and Prince Hettore Gonzaga in *Emilia Galotti*, Adelbert von Hohenburg might be the ideal romantic lover. But Thon's play connects physicality and sexuality with images of violence: Adelheit perceives Adelbert's attempt at a physical embrace as a threat, and Bertha's hysterical passion for Adelbert brings death and destruction.

The author chooses to have as her heroine a mature Adelheit instead of a naive, young, nubile Adelheit. This choice reverses the convention of bourgeois tragedy, in which a young virgin is the site of a clash between vice and virtue, duty and happiness, or familial authority and sentimental love. While the young Adelheit might have framed such a conflict, the mature Adelheit finds the conflict to be between honor and disgrace. The honorable solution is to remain with her husband and keep her vows, thus reaffirming the security of the family alliance with its stable social position. She will pay for this solution with her continued unhappiness. Her second option is to flee with Adelbert, who will make her his lover and common-law wife. This prospect, marred by disgrace and dishonor, makes her "no happier." She chooses honor, chooses the existing social system with its laws of conduct.

Adelbert bases his sense of honor on the logic of war and conflict: victory proves the cause to be a just one, and might makes right. He links honor with heroism, that is, with performance in battle. His philosophy is that the stronger overpower the weaker. In his own life, he first perceived himself as the (financially) weaker contender for Adelheit's hand—thus he lost her. Returning, he interprets his victorious survival as a sign from above that he is to win Adelheit back. He rationalizes that the word of God supersedes the word of His representatives on earth, who include the priest who married Adelheit and Robert. Adelbert's need to effect his own fate strengthens this belief. His sense of virtue has the air of contingency—it is not absolute and unalterable but context-dependent. It allows him to argue that two wrongs can make one right: because Robert married Adelheit against her will, her breaking of the marriage vows is justified.

Recent social and psychological studies of morality (e.g., Lawrence Kohlberg's) suggest several hierarchical levels of moral sophistication. Although Carol Gilligan has called into question the universality of Kohlberg's levels with respect to gender and although those levels ignore historical specificity, they nevertheless shed light on various moral positions in Thon's play. Adelheit displays what according to Kohlberg is the highest level of morality: the subordination of relationships to rules and of rules to universal principles of justice. Her concept of honor is absolute. It is based on abstract laws: her sense of duty to keep her word, her wedding vows. Refusing Adelbert's context-dependent morality, she wills a victory over her own wishes. For men, heroism was usually described as bravery and the active, successful overcoming of adversity; for women, it referred to the defense of sexual purity. Women's heroism does not conquer exterior worlds; it conquers, rather, a part of their inner world, typically their desires. Adelheit is not portrayed as the victim of an obsessive and repressive focus on sexual purity. Her refusal to leave her husband and break her promise to him is instead valued as an act of honor and strength. In the end, Adelbert has to concede that his individualistic, conflict-based understanding of honor, which ignored the rights and desires of others (Rastenberg's rights, Bertha's desires), was the cause of the resulting deaths.

The sentimental and romantic love paradigms are less stable than the social organization based on familial patterns. Thon's drama portrays excessive passion negatively; excessive passion led to the unhappy marriage of Rastenberg, whose desire made him insist on possessing Adelheit as his wife although her heart did not belong to him. Reciprocity, a necessary ingredient in love matches, cannot be willed or forced. Passion costs Bertha her dignity, her honor, and eventually her life. Her attempts to win Adelbert as husband-lover and her subsequent revenge are in vain. In addition, her character suggests the frightening possibility that as paradigms change, individuals might actually remain completely unintegrated, grounded neither by the family alliance nor by sentimental love. The dark side of the new organization of social spaces emerges. Because the sentimental and, later, romantic paradigms are highly individualistic and exclusive and yet depend on reciprocity and voluntary consent, they are difficult to realize and unreliable. When Bertha is rejected by Adelbert twice, her love turns into rage and hatred. Taking revenge, she kills Adelheit and then herself. At first glance, she resembles the villainesses of bourgeois tragedy, the lascivious noblewomen in the tradition of Marwood in *Miß Sara Sampson* and Countess Orsina in *Emilia Galotti*. Bertha is, however, a new form of social outcast. Her unrequited desire for Adelbert can no longer be socially integrated.

In this respect, she is like the male characters from Sturm und Drang drama, like Guelfo in Friedrich Maximilian Klinger's *Die Zwillinge* (1776; "The Twins") or Franz Moor in Schiller's *Die Räuber* (1781; *The Robbers*). Moreover, in the gender coordinates of the time, her desperate insistence on revenge defeminizes her. When her traditional female scheming—the seduction of Rastenberg's son, Franz, and the poisoning of Adelheit—fails, she takes the instrument of revenge, the dagger, literally into her own hands and stabs her rival. Elisabeth's horrified characterization of Bertha as "unnatural" and disgusting hints at the infringement of gender boundaries. Bertha's transgression is a metaphor of the dangerous, socially destabilizing effect of sentimental and romantic love. Furthermore, the play points to contradictions in this new paradigm. Reciprocity in love requires equality, but equality was not supported by the social structure. Gender-specific behavior patterns and value systems, for example, discouraged the open display of desire and passion in women. The play seems to voice suspicion about the sentimental-romantic love paradigm's claim of equality for the sexes. Love costs all the female characters their lives. Only that erasure brings Adelbert, Robert, and Franz to their senses. Adelbert admits the problematic nature of his passion and realizes that Adelheit's position was morally superior to his. By taking up arms in defense of his God, he hopes to repent the error of his ways and wash away his weakness in the blood of God's enemies. Robert and Adelbert assure each other of their forgiveness and friendship. Adelbert assumes the role of mentor for Franz, whom he takes with him on the Crusade.

In the negotiation of family alliance versus sentimental paradigm, the implicit political position of this drama is conservative. The drama suggests that social structures and laws are necessary for the protection and continued integration of weaker individuals, in this case women. The author has doubts both about family alliance, which disregards individual wishes and the freedom of self-determination, and about the sentimental-romantic paradigm, which is irrational, chaotic, and unpredictable and which exposes the individual to the danger of remaining totally unintegrated. The dramatic text, instead, seems to advocate enlightened rationalism: an ethical and benevolent interpretation of given laws and social structures. On the eve of the French Revolution, the play cautions against the dissolution of the things that guard against the chaos of individual desires and wishes.

Karin A. Wurst
Michigan State University

Notes

[1] Jürgen Habermas's study of the "structural transformation of the public sphere" focuses on the political potential of intense literary exchange.

[2] Romantic love that includes the celebration of sexuality would eventually replace the sentimental love paradigm. Niklas Luhmann's hypothesis that in German literature the evolution of the semantics of love was static during the eighteenth century has to be corrected (Gries). Early Enlightenment drama—for example, *Die ungleiche Heirath* (1743; *The Mésalliance*), by Luise Adelgunde Gottsched—still celebrated the traditional family alliance model. It sanctioned marriage between socially and economically compatible parties, marriage being a means for the regulation of practical interests. A new stage in the evolution of love was reached when sentimental drama emotionalized the family alliance in an attempt to combine or conflate it with

sentimental love. Lessing's *Miß Sara Sampson* is an example. With its strong foundation in friendship, sentimental love is based on exclusivity and reciprocity. In Lessing's *Emilia Galotti* the exclusion of sexuality from sentimentalism produces a crisis that eventually, by the turn of the century, leads to the romantic paradigm. Thon's play belongs in this moment of crisis that renegotiates the sentimental love paradigm.

PRINCIPAL WORKS BY
Eleonore Thon

Novels

Julie von Hirtenthal. Eine Geschichte in Briefen. 3 vols. Eisenach: Wittekind, 1780–83.

Briefe von Karl Leuckford. Eisenach: Wittekind, 1782.

Marianne von Terville. Eine Erzählung. Leipzig: n.p., 1798.

Editions of *Adelheit von Rastenberg*

Adelheit von Rastenberg. Weimar: Hoffmannische Buchhandlung, 1788.

"Adelheit von Rastenberg." *Deutsche Schaubühne* 1 (1788): 251–318.

WORKS CITED AND CONSULTED

Armstrong, Nancy, and Leonhard Tennenhouse, eds. *The Ideology of Conduct: Essays on Literature and the History of Sexuality.* New York: Methuen, 1987.

Bartels, Adolf. *Geschichte der thüringschen Literatur.* Vol. 1. Jena: Biedermann, 1938.

Becker-Cantarino, Barbara. *Der lange Weg zur Mündigkeit: Frau und Literatur (1500–1800).* Stuttgart: Metzler, 1987.

Brown, Marshall. *Preromanticism.* Stanford: Stanford UP, 1991.

Bruford, Walter. *Germany in the Eighteenth Century: The Social Background of the Literary Revival.* Cambridge: Cambridge UP, 1949.

Dawson, Ruth. "Women Communicating: Eighteenth-Century German Journals Edited by Women." *Archives et Bibliothèques de Belgique* 54 (1983): 95–111.

Eagleton, Terry. *The Rape of Clarissa: Writing, Sexuality and Class Struggle in Samuel Richardson.* Oxford: Blackwell, 1982.

Engelsing, Rolf. *Der Bürger als Leser: Lesergeschichte in Deutschland 1500–1800.* Stuttgart: Metzler, 1974.

Friedrichs, Elisabeth. *Die deutschsprachigen Schriftstellerinnen des 18. Jahrhunderts. Ein Lexikon.* Stuttgart: Metzler, 1981.

Gilligan, Carol. *In a Different Voice: Psychological Theory and Women's Development.* 1982. Cambridge: Harvard UP, 1993.

Goethe, Johann Wolfgang, and Friedrich Schiller. "Über den Dilettantismus." 1799. *Gedenkausgabe der Werke, Briefe und Gespräche: Schriften zur Literatur.* Zürich: Artemis, 1950. 729–54.

Gottsched, Luise Adelgunde Viktorie. *The Mésalliance*. Pietism in Petticoats *and Other Comedies*. Trans. and ed. Thomas Kerth and John R. Russell. Columbia: Camden, 1994: 73–138.

Greenblatt, Stephen. *Renaissance Self-Fashioning: From More to Shakespeare*. Chicago: U of Chicago P, 1980.

Gries, Jutta. *Drama Liebe: Zur Entstehungsgeschichte der modernen Liebe im Drama des 18. Jahrhunderts*. Stuttgart: Metzler, 1991.

Gross, Heinrich. *Deutschlands Dichterinen und Schriftstellerinen. Eine literarhistorische Skizze*. 2nd ed. Wien: Gerold, 1882.

Habermas, Jürgen. *Strukturwandel der Öffentlichkeit: Untersuchung zu einer Kategorie der bürgerlichen Gesellschaft*. Neuwied: Luchterhand, 1962. Trans. as *The Structural Transformation of the Public Sphere: An Inquiry into a Category of Bourgeois Society*. Trans. Thomas Burger. Cambridge: MIT P, 1989.

Hamberger, Georg, and Johann Georg Meusel. *Das gelehrte Teutschland*. 1796–1834. Hildesheim: Olms, 1965–66.

Hirsch, Marianne, Ruth Perry, and Virginia Swain. Foreword. *In the Shadow of Olympus: German Women Writers around 1800*. Ed. Katherine R. Goodman and Edith Waldstein. Albany: State U of New York P, 1992. vii–xi.

Hoff, Dagmar von. *Dramen des Weiblichen: Deutsche Dramatikerinnen um 1800*. Opladen: Westdeutscher, 1989.

Killy, Walter. *Literaturlexikon*. Vol. 11. München: Bertelsmann, 1991.

Kittler, Friedrich A. *Aufschreibesysteme 1800/1900*. München: Fink, 1985.

Kohlberg, Lawrence. *The Philosophy of Moral Development*. San Francisco: Harper, 1981.

Kord, Susanne. *Ein Blick hinter die Kulissen: Deutschsprachige Dramatikerinnen im 18. und 19. Jahrhundert*. Stuttgart: Metzler, 1992.

Koselleck, Reinhart. *Kritik und Krise: Eine Studie zur Pathogenese der bürgerlichen Welt*. 1959. Frankfurt: Suhrkamp, 1973. Trans. as *Critique and Crisis: The Enlightenment and the Origins of Political Hypocrisy*. Cambridge: MIT P, 1987.

Lamport, F. J. *German Classical Drama: Theatre, Humanity and Nation*. Cambridge: Cambridge UP, 1990.

Lange, Victor. *The Classical Age of German Literature, 1740–1815*. London: Holmes, 1982.

Leidner, Alan C. *The Impatient Muse: Germany and the Sturm und Drang*. Chapel Hill: U of North Carolina P, 1994.

Luhmann, Niklas. *Liebe als Passion. Zur Codierung von Intimität*. 3rd. ed. Frankfurt: Suhrkamp, 1983.

McCarthy, John A. "The Art of Reading and the Goals of the German Enlightenment." *Lessing Yearbook* 16 (1984): 79–94.

Rosenberg, Heidi. *Formen der Familie*. Frankfurt: Suhrkamp, 1982.

Schindel, Carl Wilhelm Otto August von. *Die deutschen Schriftstellerinnen des neunzehnten Jahrhunderts: Drei Teile in einem Band*. 1823–25. Hildesheim: Olms, 1978.

Schmid, Christian Heinrich. "Litteratur des bürgerlichen Trauerspiels." *Deutsche Monatsschrift* Dec. 1798: 282–314.

Schmidt, Henry J. *How Dramas End: Essays on the German Sturm and Drang, Büchner, Hauptmann, and Fleisser*. Ann Arbor: U of Michigan P, 1992.

Touallion, Christine. *Der deutsche Frauenroman des 18. Jahrhunderts*. Wien: Braunmüller, 1919.

Ward, Albert. *Book Production, Fiction and the German Reading Public, 1740–1800*. Oxford: Clarendon, 1974.

Wurst, Karin A. *Familiale Liebe ist die "wahre Gewalt": Zur Repräsentation der Familie in G. E. Lessings dramatischem Werk*. Amsterdam: Rodopi, 1988.

———. *Frauen und Drama im achtzehnten Jahrhundert*. Köln: Böhlau, 1991.

NOTE ON THE TEXT

In 1788, Eleonore Thon's *Adelheit von Rastenberg* appeared simultaneously as an independent book published by the Hoffmannische Buchhandlung in Weimar and as a contribution to volume 1 of *Deutsche Schaubühne*. The text used for this reprint and translation is the book, which was released and marketed by the Hoffmannische Buchhandlung for the Leipzig Easter Book Fair. The book does not bear the author's name, but anonymity was not unusual during that period. The copy we used is housed at the Deutsches Literaturarchiv Marbach. We are grateful to the archive for permission to reprint and translate the text.

In the text and the translation, the paragraph structure and centering of act and scene designations as well as of the stage directions, which we italicize, are retained. We retain the centering of the names of the characters on stage but place the names of characters speaking at the left. Obvious mistakes or misprints in the original German were corrected; these relatively minor corrections are reflected in the translation.

Because the play was not reprinted until now, there exists little critical discussion—especially in English—about Eleonore Thon and her works. We have therefore added to the works-cited list reading selections that provide information about eighteenth-century literature and culture in Germany.

GFP and KAW

ELEONORE THON

Adelheit von Rastenberg

A Tragedy in Five Acts

Characters

Robert von Rastenberg   ⎫
Adelbert von Hohenburg ⎬   knights
                               ⎭
Adelheit, Robert's wife
Elisabeth, her confidante
Bertha, the widowed Countess von Wildenau
Franz, Rastenberg's illegitimate son, nineteen years old
Wenzel, Hohenburg's squire and confidant
Curt, in Rastenberg's service
A hermit
Numerous squires and armed men
Bertha's entourage

The action takes place in Franconia during the Crusades;
it begins in the morning and lasts three days.

Preface

The subject of this tragedy is taken from a true old German family chronicle. Only the names have been changed and minor details added, in order to condense the events, thus adding to the play's vitality, and also to provide better motivation, thus increasing the events' truth and tragic import. Since dramatists have always taken the liberty of adjusting historical events to fit their plans, there should be no objection to changes of this kind, so long as they have a purpose. And they do have a purpose if they have an effect.

At the Leipzig Easter Fair, 1788

ACT 1

*Very early in the morning, in a small wood
not far from Rastenberg's castle.*

Scene 1

Hohenburg, Wenzel

HOHENBURG: She's coming here?

WENZEL: Yes, my lord. I discovered that it's her habit to
walk here alone every morning while her husband
is out hunting. And no wonder. How inviting this
place is! These firs make a perfect hideaway for lovers—and this thicket (*looking around*). Look! What's
stirring there?— There she is.— Withdraw, my lord,
so that seeing me may prepare her to see you.

HOHENBURG: How my heart is pounding! It didn't pound
this hard the first time I showed my visor to the
enemy.

WENZEL: I believe it, good master, I believe it! And a
beautiful woman is the most dangerous of enemies.

Scene 2

Wenzel, Adelheit

*Adelheit enters slowly, lost in melancholy.
Wenzel steps in front of her.*

WENZEL: Good day, noble lady. Do you still know me?

ADELHEIT (*startled*): Whom do I see?— Wenzel? You? Here?

WENZEL: In the flesh! But why so sad, dear lady? You should smile; I have a joyful message for you.

ADELHEIT (*hurriedly*): From your lord?— (*Aside.*) O my heart, how you betray yourself!

WENZEL (*gives her a letter*): Here, take it.

ADELHEIT (*more hurriedly than before*): So he's alive? Where is he?

WENZEL: Perhaps nearer than you think.— But I beg you, read it.

*Trembling, Adelheit reads the letter, hides it,
and sighs.*

WENZEL: Surely you're not going to answer such a precious letter with just a sigh.

ADELHEIT: How can I do otherwise? Don't you know that I am Rastenberg's wife?

WENZEL: And Hohenburg's beloved.—

ADELHEIT: What do you mean?—

WENZEL: What my lord will now tell you himself. (*Exits.*)

Scene 3

Adelheit, Hohenburg

HOHENBURG (*hurries forward and embraces her*): It's true, Adelheit. You are still my soul's beloved.

ADELHEIT (*embarrassed*): Adelbert!— Sir Knight!— What are you doing!— I am no longer free.

HOHENBURG: Why not, Adelheit?— The bonds of marriage couldn't chain your heart; it remained mine even in Rastenberg's embrace.— Or did your brother lie to me; was I deceived by the letter from you he brought me in the Holy Land?— Or did your hardhearted, greedy father not force you to accept Rastenberg, the richer one? Was he (*with some bitterness*) perhaps your own choice?

ADELHEIT: If you did speak with my brother, did read my letter, then don't misunderstand me or the truth. For eleven months I resisted the pleas and threats of my father, until he finally dragged me to the altar. "Choose now," he said, his eyes rolling dreadfully, "choose either Rastenberg or my curse!" I threw myself at Rastenberg's feet and begged for my freedom, but he said that he was not free himself, was a prisoner of his love for me. My father forced our hands together and so (*sighing*)—we became man and wife. My brother became so angry at Father

9

that he took up the Cross without telling him and vowed not to rest until he had found you and given you that letter.

HOHENBURG: He kept his vow, the noble man!— And he did more than promised; he eased my pain and sparked my resolve to come back and tear you from Rastenberg's arms.

ADELHEIT: That sounds like my brother's youthful fervor. But where is he?— Didn't he return with you?

HOHENBURG (*taking her hand*): No, my dearest!—but he sends to you this handclasp.

ADELHEIT: He's still alive?—

HOHENBURG: Yes, dear lady, in a better world, where he is receiving the reward for his bravery.

ADELHEIT: O God! So he is gone—and my father, who grieved at the loss of his only son, is gone, too. Lucky for him!— But tell me, Adelbert, when did my brother die, and how?

HOHENBURG: It's been a whole year now since he died a hero's death at my side. As he lay dying, he clasped my hand and said, "This is for Adelheit, and she is yours." His last words have echoed through the depths of my soul. In the heat of battle and the hush of prayer, waking and dreaming, I hear: "Adelheit is yours." My courage grew stronger; I fought my way through the most terrible dangers; and now, Adelheit, look upon the victor at your feet, gaze lovingly at him, and be the reward for his bravery.

ADELHEIT: Stand up, Hohenburg; what can I do for you?

HOHENBURG: Flee with me to Thuringia!

Adelheit recoils.

HOHENBURG: Don't be alarmed, my love! My sister, an honest, upright woman, who was once herself the victim of unhappy love, awaits us there; she'll take us in. We'll—

ADELHEIT (*interrupting him*): It was exactly four years ago today, Hohenburg, that I had to vow to be faithful to my husband—I've been most unhappy ever since. Don't ask me to perjure myself as well.

HOHENBURG: A vow taken under duress is no vow at all! Look at the omen from heaven! Look at me here, escaped from danger. Look at me here, guided across deserts and oceans to you, my beloved, by the hand of the One who joined our hearts long before a priest represented His divinity at the altar. The One who rules above us Himself is opening my arms for you—follow me to Thuringia.

ADELHEIT: Let me go, Adelbert, let me go!

HOHENBURG (*holding her tight*): No, dearest, I won't let you go. You are my wife, if the voice of heaven

11

speaks louder than a priest's blessing—my beloved, if your heart isn't deceitful and you wish to understand what mine is saying—my inheritance, if you still honor your brother's last wish.

ADELHEIT (*trying to free herself*): Let me go, for God's sake, let me go; we're not safe here.

HOHENBURG (*hurriedly*): In the name of the Almighty who determined our love and our fate! I won't release you until you tell me where I can see you again.

ADELHEIT (*stammering*): Well—tonight, then—at the hermit's hut.

HOHENBURG: Adelheit, Adelheit, don't betray me!

ADELHEIT: Oh Adelbert! O heavenly saints!

> *They exit to opposite sides, Adelheit in*
> *great haste.*

Scene 4

A hall in Rastenberg's castle.

Elisabeth

ELISABETH (*nervously pacing*): What can be taking Adelheit so long?— Hohenburg's castle isn't far— What if the rumor about his return is true, and he has found her—oh—I'm so frightened!

Scene 5

Adelheit, Elisabeth

ADELHEIT (*rushes through the door and into Elisabeth's arms*): Oh Elisabeth!— I have seen him, I have seen my soul mate!

ELISABETH: Whom— Hohenburg?

ADELHEIT: In person, and I am no happier. Often, as I wandered alone through the little forest, I thought to myself, If you could just once encounter his spirit, things would be easier for you, you would be more at peace. My God! Now I've seen him, heard his voice! But it didn't calm my heart.

ELISABETH: Dear Adelheit, you're beside yourself.

ADELHEIT: You are right. (*With her hand on her heart.*) There's a frightful turmoil here. Help me pray, my girl, that this storm may ease.

ELISABETH: Where did you meet Hohenburg? What did he say to you?

ADELHEIT: Quiet! I think I hear my husband. Follow me to my chamber; there you'll learn everything.

Both exit.

Scene 6

Rastenberg, Franz *(coming from the hunt)*

RASTENBERG: So Sir Hohenburg has been back for two weeks already?

FRANZ: Yes, Father.

RASTENBERG: Are you sure?

FRANZ: I'm sure. And besides, when I was returning from the hunt yesterday evening, I saw Wenzel not far from the castle.

RASTENBERG *(with some agitation)*: Did he recognize you?

FRANZ: Oh, as well as I him; but he disappeared into the bushes right away. You had better keep an eye on your wife.— Hohenburg could become dangerous to you.

RASTENBERG *(with forced composure)*: I'm not afraid of him. But still, your advice is good.

FRANZ: Take it then, Father, for *(somewhat timidly)* Adelheit has never loved you.

RASTENBERG: That's the sad truth, Franz. This woman whom I loved to distraction, whom I still adore, makes me more miserable than I can say!—

FRANZ *(even more timidly)*: Forgive me, Father—but I'm afraid—you deserve this for what you did to my mother.

14

RASTENBERG (*angrily*): What I did to your mother?—Rogue, do you know what you're saying!

FRANZ (*more boldly*): Forgive me, Father, but wasn't my mother of noble birth? Am I not living proof of her tenderness toward you?— (*Sighs deeply.*) You cast her out!

RASTENBERG (*composed*): Franz, you've given me reproachful looks about this matter before, and I remained silent. Now that you've been bold enough to speak out, it's my duty to tell you the secret story of your mother. It's short, but it will teach you much and vindicate me. Your mother was of noble French blood; she was beautiful but poor, and that's why my father would not approve of our marriage. I loved her with all the ardor of youth and could not bring myself to leave her. She swore to be eternally faithful to me as well, and so I promised that if she remained worthy of me, I would lead her to the altar after my father's death. We thus felt we were united in God's eyes, and you were born. For two years we managed to keep your birth secret, until somebody told your grandfather. In his anger he forced me to join the Crusades, where I was supposed to atone for my sin through bravery. When we parted, I gave your mother money and reminded her to remain true to her oath; and as God is my witness, if she had not betrayed me with her unfaithfulness, she, and no other, would be my wife today. But what did she do? While I faced danger and death fighting for honor and glory, she reveled in lust and forgot me in favor of a spineless coward who never showed the enemy anything but his back and managed to escape my wrath. My father died; I returned home after eight years, discovered her wrongdoing, and banished her to a nunnery, from which she escaped not long ago. For five years after that I avoided the entire female race—if only I had fled it forever!—but I saw Adelheit and was irresistibly drawn to her; her father strongly encouraged my passion—the rest you know, don't you? So tell me, do you still think I treated your mother unjustly?

FRANZ (*with a kind of noble indignation*): Well, Father, if she could act that way, then she herself severed the bond that held you to her. But still—(*after a short pause*) why must I, who am innocent, atone for the guilty one? Why must I be mocked by the whole world as a bastard?

RASTENBERG (*moved*): Have I not sought to rectify the injustice of your birth through the most loving care? Did I not carry you into this castle in my arms? Have you not grown up here under my supervision without the slightest want? Do I not still do much for you?

FRANZ: Much, but not everything. In spite of all your good deeds toward me, I am still a bastard. If you could only feel how any spark of courage in my soul is doused by the awful thought "You're a bastard"— oh, Father, if you could only feel it, you'd take pity on me.

RASTENBERG (*deeply moved*): Franz—my son—do you wish to break my heart?

FRANZ: No, but I'd like to move your paternal heart to take pity on me.

RASTENBERG: You have succeeded. What more do you want from me?

FRANZ (*kneeling*): Your name, Father, your noble name.

RASTENBERG (*lifting him up*): You shall have it, Son, before God and the world. I will outfit you as a knight, and if indeed my wife bears me no children, you shall be heir to everything over which magnates and feudal lords have no claim.

FRANZ (*joyfully*): Really, Father, do you mean it?

RASTENBERG: I do.

FRANZ: Then give me your right hand as a knight's pledge.

RASTENBERG (*gives him his hand*): A Rastenberg has never broken his word, remember that.

FRANZ: Oh, Father! Only now do I feel how your blood courses through my veins. May both you and my future deeds be blessed.

17

RASTENBERG (*aside*): How strongly his joy affects him. (*To Franz.*) Go, my son, rest a while, and ask that Adelheit be sent to me.

FRANZ (*embracing his father*): At once, Father. (*Exits.*)

Scene 7

Rastenberg (*alone*)

RASTENBERG: So my heart is not yet completely impoverished! Even if I do lack the affection of my wife, I have a son who loves me, whose one and only joy is that he belongs to me. Oh, may fatherly love soon fill this heart so completely that there will no longer be any room for unhappy longing for that ungrateful woman!

Scene 8

Rastenberg, Adelheit

ADELHEIT: Here I am, Robert. What do you have to say to me?

RASTENBERG: There is much, very much, I would like to tell you, but (*looking into her eyes*) you have been crying again. I guess you will never show me a happy countenance.

ADELHEIT: It seems I was not born to be happy.

RASTENBERG: Don't say that! Every creature is born to be happy; it's just that you spurn happiness as well as my love. Adelheit, Adelheit! How much have I already suffered on your account!— At least try to gladden my heart with the semblance of affection, try to pretend some tenderness. Can't you do that? After all, you are my wife.

ADELHEIT: Your ideas about a wife seem to have been debased by Franz's mother. (*With dignity.*) Remember, I am a German woman and not capable of any deception.

RASTENBERG (*angrily*): Say, rather, an ungrateful woman! (*Composed.*) But patience (*stroking her face softly*), I shall not be slave to this attraction forever. Let us talk about something else. I told you that I have to leave for Würzburg tomorrow; when I return, I want to experience some domestic joy and have Franz declared my legitimate son. That meets with your approval?

ADELHEIT: Why shouldn't it? You are the master and can do what you like.

RASTENBERG: I'm afraid that answer doesn't come from your heart. You don't like the boy much; you think he's deceptive. But you do him wrong. Just now I had a touching encounter with him; he opened his heart to me completely. That heart is totally genuine and is now filled with the kind of courage that will bring honor to my name. (*Sighing.*) Besides, I dare not hope that you will ever give me a more precious son.

ADELHEIT: I approve of everything. Robert, believe me, you are wrong to doubt the sincerity of my words.

RASTENBERG: I will doubt no longer. Many thanks! (*Adelheit starts to go.*) Another thing. Did you know that Hohenburg is home again?

ADELHEIT (*with agitation*): Yes—I know.

RASTENBERG (*noticing her agitation*): Then—even if your heart tells you otherwise—you will avoid seeing him.

ADELHEIT: I'll avoid anything that might disgrace you and me.

RASTENBERG: Farewell then, until we see each other again. Now I want to make preparations with my companions for the trip tomorrow.

> *Adelheit, moved, gives Rastenberg her*
> *hand, which he kisses while giving*
> *her a penetrating look; then he exits.*

Scene 9

Adelheit

ADELHEIT: I will do nothing that might disgrace you and me. That means not seeing Adelbert, not fleeing with him. But I must keep my word and speak with him tonight at the hermit's; for if he felt deceived, how I would have to fear his rage. (*After a brief pause.*) Oh, I must, must see him again! (*Looking toward heaven.*) May the benevolent being who watches over us poor, weak mortals guide my steps and teach me how to conquer myself.

ACT 2

Toward evening, in the wood.

Scene 1

Franz

FRANZ (*alone, pacing nervously back and forth*): Why is it that I'm suddenly filled with such anxiety? I was so happy, so relieved just this morning, relishing the thought of my impending happiness, and now— What if this strange feeling is a premonition, a premonition of some grievous event that threatens to destroy my dreams of happiness. (*Pause.*) Oh! there are examples enough of those who laughed in the morning only to weep by nightfall. Who knows if there aren't yet tears to be shed on my pillow today! (*Stands in silent contemplation.*)

Scene 2

Franz, Bertha

BERTHA VON WILDENAU (*enters wearing a veil; observes Franz for a few moments*): At last I meet you.

FRANZ: Who's that? (*Catches sight of her.*) God be with you, noble lady! May I ask—

BERTHA: Don't you recognize my voice anymore, Franz?

FRANZ: It enchants my ear, and it seems I've heard it before; but I don't know to whom it belongs.

BERTHA: Doesn't it remind you of a song you heard a few years ago at one of Rastenberg's grand banquets?

FRANZ (*hastily*): The song of lovely Bertha? (*His hand on his heart.*) Oh, it penetrated deeply here!— Heavens, is it really you, Bertha?

BERTHA (*throwing back her veil*): Judge for yourself.

FRANZ (*gazing at her in wonder*): So it is, beautiful Bertha herself!

BERTHA: I've often looked for you here. Why is it that I never encountered you before today?

FRANZ: You've looked for me, noble countess? How could you lower yourself so far?

BERTHA: What do you mean, lower? Unhappy people are closely related, the two of us also.

FRANZ: That I've been unhappy up to now I know all too well; but I didn't know that you were unhappy, too.

24

BERTHA: Well, now you know that I need a friend, an ally like yourself. The noblest, bravest knights in Franconia once sought my hand; but the heart is a stubborn thing, and I rejected all those who wooed me in favor of the one who didn't; and that unworthy man was Hohenburg.

FRANZ (*with amazement*): Hohenburg?

BERTHA: You heard right.— I tried to conceal my passion for him, to the point that I became ill. My uncle, who loved me like a daughter after my parents died, realized that my sickness lay in my heart and succeeded in drawing the secret out of me. He made Hohenburg an extremely attractive offer of betrothal to me, but (*with grim anger*) Hohenburg rejected me in favor of Adelheit, me, whom all adored!— This insult brought me to my senses, and I sought revenge, but Hohenburg escaped by going to Palestine. Adelheit had to marry your father, and so my soul again grew still. Old Count Wildenau sought my hand soon thereafter; I accepted, don't ask me why, suffered for a few years at his side, and then gave thanks for the death that parted us. In my lonely, widowed state, my love for the ungrateful Hohenburg awoke again; two weeks ago he returned, I sent him greetings, he hardly responded. One of my acquaintances reiterated my uncle's earlier offer of betrothal to him, and (*striking herself on the forehead*)—oh, that I had to suffer this, this indignity!—he rejected me a second time. As long as an Adelheit lives, he said, no Bertha will attract me.

FRANZ: Incredible! How did that affect you, Countess?

BERTHA: As it was bound to. A poisonous vapor from hell enveloped my love and turned it into hatred, red-hot hatred thirsting for revenge. (*Confidingly.*) Franz, wouldn't you like to do me a favor and become the tool for my revenge?

FRANZ (*backing away*): What do you mean, Countess?

BERTHA: That without giving me away, you tell your father how Hohenburg plans to flee with his wife, and that for this purpose the couple has a rendezvous tonight at the hermit's hut.

FRANZ (*enraged*): Ha, so that's where her sacred steps lead! (*Controlling himself.*) But dear Countess, from whom did you hear this?

BERTHA: From the tender couple themselves. For some time now I've been taking walks here, and it happened this morning that I was strolling behind these bushes, heard the two of them talking, and learned everything from their own lips.

FRANZ: Thank you, lovely Countess! Poor, deceived father! You seem destined to be the plaything of unfaithful women.— My mother betrayed you, and you rejected her only to be betrayed a thousand times worse. I feel truly sorry for you, but I want to prove to you that I am worthy of being named your son. I want to avenge your honor, want to—

BERTHA (*interrupting him*): Don't waste your time dreaming, dear youth; take action. But first, give me your hand to pledge our revenge.

FRANZ: Here, Countess.

BERTHA: There. Now go and find your father; but you'll have to pretend nothing's wrong if you see Adelheit before her rendezvous. And (*looking at him lovingly*) you mustn't go along to the hideaway if your father wants to surprise his wife there.

FRANZ: Why not?

BERTHA (*as before*): Because I say so. But tomorrow around noon I'll steal back here, and don't you fail to show up. (*Sighs.*) There's still so much weighing on my heart. (*Starts to go.*)

FRANZ (*stopping her*): One more thing, lovely Countess! Soon I will be declared Rastenberg's legitimate son. Then I'll no longer be that poor nameless fool who once shyly listened for your sweet voice.— Then I'll be bold enough to lay claim to your heart. Will you grant it to me?

BERTHA: This heart will be given only with this hand, and both (*looking at Franz meaningfully*) will belong only to him who takes revenge on Hohenburg.

FRANZ (*delighted*): Then in the name of Saint Kilian, you are all mine, for I (*slapping his sword*) shall avenge you.

BERTHA: Bravo, Franz, bravo! Take care of yourself! Until we meet again. (*Throws him a kiss and exits hurriedly.*)

Scene 3

Franz

FRANZ (*looking after her*): What was that—a seductive apparition, or was it really she? (*Stands for several minutes, as if in a dream.*) You beautiful, sweet woman! So you would be mine, with all your charms and all your riches? But at what price? (*Musing.*) But yes, by avenging her I also avenge my poor deceived father; and that's no less than my duty. (*Exits.*)

Scene 4

*Night, a thicket, in the background a hut,
from which emerge Hohenburg and a hermit.*

Hohenburg, Hermit

HERMIT: Think carefully about what you are doing, Knight. The laws of the church are holy, and He above us is their defender.

HOHENBURG: Be just, honorable old man, and tell me who is the greater criminal, the one who misuses the laws of the church to satisfy a deranged passion or the one who trespasses against these laws only because he sees no other way to rescue the unfortunate casualty of that passion?

HERMIT: Both are culpable.

HOHENBURG: You are too strict, Father; heaven is more forgiving.

HERMIT: Does it not clearly violate a commandment to steal the wife of your neighbor?

HOHENBURG: I am not stealing; Adelheit is mine; I am simply reclaiming a possession that Rastenberg forcefully took away in my absence.

HERMIT: How clever humans are in putting a good face on their crimes. Sir Knight! Once again I warn you: think about what you're doing! The time may come when you regret your hasty deed, only it will be too late.

HOHENBURG: This deed is no hasty one; I've been planning it for a long time.

HERMIT: So much the worse.

HOHENBURG: I hear you condemn me with a cold heart, in which anguished love will never find refuge.

HERMIT (*extremely moved*): With a cold heart? I wish to God that were the truth! I, too, was young once; I, too, was impetuous and weak. I know how the most unhappy of all passions can drive men crazy, how its sweetness can turn to bitter gall.

HOHENBURG (*approaching him reverently*): You know that, too? Then have pity and forgive me.

The hermit sighs deeply.

Scene 5

The preceding, Adelheit, Elisabeth

HOHENBURG: Have you come, my dearest?

ADELHEIT (*in a decisive voice*): Yes, Adelbert, I've come to tell you that I love you more than anything, that my heart will always be yours, but also that it must always remain free of evil deeds, that I do not want to transgress against Rastenberg, that I intend to endure the remaining dark days of my life at his side.

HERMIT: Bless you, my child, for the virtue that is uttered from your lips.

HOHENBURG: So you want to endure? want to sweeten the life of the monster who so embitters ours?— Adelheit—you can't be serious.

ADELHEIT: But I am, Knight, I am—

HOHENBURG (*with anguish*): Then you've never loved me; your letter was a sham; your brother lied, and I—I was a fool to believe either of you.

ADELHEIT: I swear to you on the ashes of my dead brother, do not misjudge me! My last earthly thought will be of you, and in that better world I will be yours eternally; in this one, however (*turning away her face*), we must part.

HOHENBURG (*looking at her tenderly*): Part! Adelheit can speak this word so calmly?

ADELHEIT (*aside*): Heaven, give me strength! (*To Hohenburg.*) I must, Adelbert; duty demands it.

HOHENBURG: Duty is cold! Follow the call of warm love!

ADELHEIT: Its call is sweet; but I cannot, may not succumb to it.

HOHENBURG: I respect your noble-mindedness; but Rastenberg doesn't deserve it; and if the law makes you a sinner for leaving him, then I'll take this sin upon myself. You are innocent.

ADELHEIT: Allow me to remain so.

HOHENBURG: You shall! Only come, and let us triumph over our fate.

ADELHEIT: Sometimes it is more noble to submit to one's fate than to triumph over it. Farewell, Adelbert; be a man. (*Tries to leave.*)

HOHENBURG (*restraining her*): Dearest, beloved, I beg you.

HERMIT: Sir Knight, will you allow this woman to teach you a lesson in constancy?

31

HOHENBURG: What does constancy mean for a woman? Patience and resignation in the face of misfortune. But for a man it means the courage and strength to uphold his convictions and to overcome misfortune. With my resoluteness I can break your chains. Come, dearest, my squires are waiting with the horses not far from here. Let's be off to Thuringia.

ADELHEIT (*trying to get loose*): Adelbert! Do you wish to ruin me entirely?

ELISABETH (*who until now has stood motionless with bowed head, suddenly looks around*): What's that? (*Noise from offstage.*) We are betrayed!

ADELHEIT (*fainting into Hohenburg's arms*): I am lost!

Scene 6

The preceding, Rastenberg, armed men,
torch bearers

RASTENBERG (*to Adelheit*): Ha! Adulterous woman! You here!

HOHENBURG (*with dignity*): Yes, here, in the arms of the man who had earlier claim to her than you.

RASTENBERG (*in extreme anger*): How dare you! Prove your claim, draw your sword.

ADELHEIT (*recovering somewhat, rushes from Hohenburg's arms to Elisabeth's*): Robert, I am innocent.

HERMIT (*almost simultaneously with Adelheit*): Yes, in God's name, she is innocent.

ELISABETH: Holy Mother, protect her!

Hohenburg and Rastenberg start to duel; the hermit steps between them.

HERMIT: In the name of the Almighty, peace!

Both lower their swords.

RASTENBERG (*contemplating the hermit*): Who are you to demand peace? A procurer in holy garb?

HERMIT: My duty is to condone and to forgive, but I do more: I pity you (*in a trembling voice*). Knight, Knight, your fate affects me more than you know.

RASTENBERG (*shaken*): The sound of that voice!— It penetrates my very soul.— (*To his men.*) Take the woman away.

HOHENBURG (*threatening*): If anything happens to her, you shall pay with your lives!

RASTENBERG (*defiant*): I am the one who commands her— I—

Adelheit is helped away.

ELISABETH (*exiting*): Oh, had we only stayed away from this place!

The hermit enters his hut with gestures of lamentation.

Scene 7

Hohenburg, Rastenberg

HOHENBURG (*to Rastenberg, more calmly*): Let us have reverence for this consecrated place and its pious inhabi-
tant. At dawn tomorrow we shall finish this feud in
the alder grove. Until then, I beseech you, spare your
suffering wife. She is innocent.

RASTENBERG: We shall see. Until tomorrow, Hohenburg!

HOHENBURG: Until tomorrow.

Both sheathe their swords.

ACT 3

Morning, in Rastenberg's hall.

Scene 1

Franz

FRANZ (*alone, sitting at a table, his head on his hand*): How I long for this contest to be over! What if my father falls, and with him my patron, my name! Oh, may the holy powers protect him!—

Scene 2

Franz, Rastenberg

RASTENBERG (*enters, in his armor*): Have you been waiting for me, Franz?

FRANZ (*rising to approach him*): With bated breath, Father! Did you prevail?

RASTENBERG: Neither of us did.

FRANZ: How can that be, Father?

RASTENBERG: The strangest duel I ever fought, for sure! We fought unusually long and with a fury that seemed to redouble our strength; but still, neither was able to better the other. In the end we took this to be providence, came to terms, and Hohenburg swore a holy oath that Adelheit was innocent. It's true that he wanted to escape with her, but she had decided to meet him at the hermit's hut only to dissuade him from his plan.

FRANZ (*confused*): You mean she really is innocent?

RASTENBERG: Yes, dear Franz, rejoice with me. Since Adelheit doesn't want to leave me out of love for Hohenburg, there's still hope that with time her heart will soften toward me. I was just on my way up to her to throw myself at her feet and ask her forgiveness for being so suspicious and unfeeling; but the tower guard said that she had been crying all night, had just fallen asleep exhausted, and that Elisabeth had asked that she not be disturbed. I can delay no longer, however; my men are all waiting outside. So I ask you to go to her as soon as she awakens and report the outcome of the duel. Tell her that I am keeping her in the tower not out of anger now but rather for her own safety, and that I pledge to spend the rest of my life making amends for my heartlessness. So that she believes you, take her this ring as a token of my remorse and reconciliation. Franz, are you listening?

FRANZ (*still in confusion*): Yes—I hear you.

RASTENBERG: Speak to her with all the warmth at your command. I'll reward you for this favor. Now, accompany me for a ways. (*Exits.*)

FRANZ (*exiting*): This does not bode well for my fortunes.

Scene 3

In the wood.

Bertha

BERTHA (*alone*): For such an eager lover Franz is certainly taking his time. Can it be that he's deceiving me? (*Thinking.*) But—why should I be afraid of such a thing? Unless it's because I'm deceiving him myself, pretending feelings for him that I don't have. You poor boy, I wish I could love you, you'd be worth it; but this moody heart has been capable of loving (*emphatically*) only one—and this love has transformed itself into all-consuming hatred. Unhappy Bertha, inner peace has been banished forever from your breast. Not one of life's joys remains for me, and I have no business here other than revenge (*angrily*), a revenge that will plunge me along with my victim into the most horrid abyss. (*Composing herself.*)

But calm, poor martyred heart; Franz shouldn't find you in such a heated state. (*Paces back and forth while glancing about wildly.*)

Scene 4

Bertha, Franz

FRANZ: What's the matter, lovely Countess? You seem upset.

BERTHA: What do you expect, after you left me here waiting for so long?

FRANZ (*kissing her hand*): Forgive me, dearest, I had to accompany my father for a ways.

BERTHA: Is he gone?— I heard that the duel had a happy outcome.

FRANZ: That's just what I wanted to tell you. How did you know it already?

BERTHA: Good Franz, I have my spies everywhere. You still have some matters to report to me, though. How did your father respond?

FRANZ: He was happy about his wife's innocence, which Adelbert had sworn to him, and he charged me with asking her to forgive him and with keeping her locked up in the tower for her protection until he returns.

BERTHA (*mockingly*): And of course you'll do it?

FRANZ (*with some trepidation*): Let Bertha decide.

BERTHA: That's the way the man must answer who hopes to win Bertha's hand. Listen, Franz, I'll decide quickly. You're to carry out your father's orders, but you're also to give Adelheit this medicine without her knowledge. (*Gives him a powder.*)

FRANZ (*shocked, looks at her questioningly*): Countess—this is poison.

BERTHA (*in a friendly tone*): No, it isn't; it's a sedative. It will make her feel better.

FRANZ: Countess, don't talk to me like a child. I'm a man.

BERTHA (*seriously*): Then act like a man. Kill her with this powder.

FRANZ: That's not how a man kills. (*Gesturing toward his sword.*) This is his instrument for killing.

BERTHA: Yes, if a man is dealing with men; but for a weak woman, it's best to disguise death. Wouldn't it be stupid to murder Adelheit with your sword? There'd be an awful uproar, and your father would suspect us. This poison works silently; she might even have taken it herself last night, when she was so apprehensive. This deception will protect us; your father will forget the ungrateful woman and give you his entire heart, his entire fortune. Hohenburg will be in despair about Adelheit's death, and I—I will be avenged. (*Taking his hand tenderly.*) And we two will be happy together.

FRANZ (*in astonishment*): What a hideous scheme!—

BERTHA: What are you saying? Did you not make a pact with me to seek revenge?

FRANZ: Revenge, yes, but not underhanded villainy.

BERTHA (*angrily*): Wretch! How dare you say that to me! But it serves me right, choosing someone like you (*disdainfully*) to be my confidant.

FRANZ: Don't be angry. I'll keep my promise; but I never agreed to what you're asking me to do now. Why should Adelheit die if she's innocent? Let's take our revenge on Hohenburg alone. It won't be long until I'm really a nobleman; then I'll challenge him to a duel for insulting your honor. Your love will give my arm strength; he will die.

BERTHA: How can you be sure of that? (*Crying.*) Couldn't his sword just as easily strike you down? Haven't I suffered enough blows? Is losing you to make me even more miserable?

FRANZ: Dearest lady! Don't take advantage of my weak nature!—

BERTHA: Oh, you're not weak. You can watch me cry and not be moved.

FRANZ: God forgive me, I can't!— (*Wipes away his tears.*) See, this is the power you have over me.

BERTHA (*passionately*): Let me kiss away your tears.

FRANZ (*lovingly*): Bertha, Bertha, I vowed to be your avenger and am now myself becoming your victim. What a sweet, seductive woman you are! (*Embraces her.*)

BERTHA (*as before*): Am I? And still you resist me!—

FRANZ (*pulling himself together*): Not you, not your powerful charms.— You've captivated all my senses; it's only my conscience you haven't yet conquered. (*Lovingly.*) Dear, dear Bertha, abandon this idea; don't make me a criminal.

BERTHA: Very well! Let Adelheit live, and let this medicine be for me! If I can't be avenged by Franz, for whom alone I wanted to live, then let me be avenged by death! (*Takes back the powder; starts to go.*)

FRANZ (*upset*): Stop, Countess, what are you doing? Don't drive me mad.

BERTHA: Somebody who was so full of reason a second ago will not go mad that quickly. You'll forget me soon enough. (*With extreme affection.*) Franz, Franz, you couldn't tolerate my tears, and now you're going to let me die?—

FRANZ (*even more upset*): You shall not die. The world will have to end first. Give me the powder.

BERTHA: No, it's for me. Farewell.—

FRANZ (*tears it from her hand*): No, it's for— (*Stops suddenly and stares at Bertha.*)

BERTHA: For Adelheit?

FRANZ (*stammering*): Well, yes, then. Just tell me when I will see you again.

BERTHA (*joyfully*): Tomorrow morning at my castle. It's only an hour away; (*affectionately*) my love will guide you.

FRANZ: Women, women, what you can turn us into! We're either noble or ruthless, depending on how your passions touch our souls.

BERTHA: Don't tarry any longer, my dear one.— Keep your word, and you're mine; but if you deceive me, remember, there's more of this medicine.— (*Embraces Franz. Exiting, aside.*) I'd better listen to what this little boy is up to.

Scene 5

Franz

FRANZ (*remains standing in deep thought*): It seems I too have become the plaything of the alluring sex. Bertha, Bertha, how can you be so affectionate and so heartless at the same time! Now I understand the dread I felt yesterday. This frightful turmoil in my heart signifies both your love and my doom. But take courage! I'm still only wavering on the precipice of disaster; I haven't yet sealed my fate as a scoundrel;

the tempest in Bertha's soul may yet subside—will subside, since she loves me. No, Adelheit, you shall not be sacrificed, but—I can't sacrifice the countess for you either. (*Thinking to himself.*) I'll have to resort to treachery—it's a demeaning step, to be sure, but is there a better one? Do I have a friend who can advise me, who can reach out to save this poor soul from drowning?— If only my father were still here!— (*As he starts to leave, Curt enters.*) Curt, you've come just at the right moment.

Scene 6

Franz, Curt

CURT: You're here, Franz?

FRANZ: As you see, Curt. You have always been devoted to me; will you remain so?

CURT: Do you doubt me, Franz?

FRANZ: Then promise to do something for me.

CURT: If I can.

FRANZ: You can. Promise me.

CURT (*gives him his hand*): I promise.

FRANZ: You're on watch tonight at the tower. At midnight Adelheit will escape with Elisabeth, and you're not to prevent it.

CURT: What reason do you have to help them escape?

FRANZ: The most important one in the world. You'll learn everything, only now there's no time to explain.

CURT: What will happen to me when your father returns?

FRANZ: You'll have to flee as well, of course. So that there will be no unpleasantness for you. Take this bag with money. Father gave it to me this morning; you'll find enough in it to live comfortably for a while. Before long there will be some great changes in my life; and then I'll call you back into my service, where you'll always have an easy berth. But go, before it strikes twelve.

CURT: Oh, I don't want to stand guard at all; I want to be gone.

FRANZ: So much the better. (*Emphatically.*) I shall keep my word, Curt, as an honorable man; but if you're a scoundrel and betray me, then—tremble.

CURT: Trust me, Franz. Have I ever betrayed you? Farewell!

FRANZ: Farewell, Curt, and think on what I have said! (*Exits.*)

Scene 7

Curt

CURT (*alone*): If you betray me, then tremble.— Hm! One doesn't tremble so easily from a distance. I'd better

44

have a word with Countess Bertha. (*Walks toward the place where Bertha exited; she meets him.*)

Scene 8

Curt, Bertha

CURT: I was just about to look for you in the hunting lodge.

BERTHA: There is no need, Curt. I heard everything.

CURT: You heard everything your confidant said here?

BERTHA: Everything.— Ha, that snake! I thought something was wrong; that's why I waited behind these bushes.

CURT: I warned you not to confide in this weakling, didn't I?— But what will you do now? I heard from one of the squires that Hohenburg is arming himself for tonight. Presumably he caught wind of this business and wants to take Adelheit into his protection.

BERTHA: What!— Hohenburg is arming himself to free her?— (*With mocking laughter.*) Let him come, Curt, let him come! I have a friend left who is truer than all of you. (*Pulling a small dagger from her bosom.*) Look, this is where he sleeps, but he'll awaken— awaken with a vengeance and open a bloody way for me out of this labyrinth of shame and treachery.

CURT: With your courage you don't need me anymore.

BERTHA: Ha, this courage inflames my every nerve. (*Throws him some money.*) Farewell! (*With wild gestures.*) But tonight at midnight, think of me; that's when I'll be howling my bridal song for Adelheit. (*Exits.*)

Scene 9

Curt

CURT (*alone*): Go ahead, take your full measure of sin, what do I care. My service is up, and my pockets are full. (*Exits.*)

Scene 10

A room in the tower.

Adelheit, Elisabeth

ADELHEIT (*sitting on a bed*): My husband wished to see me?

ELISABETH: That's what the tower guard said.

ADELHEIT: Why did you let me sleep so long?

ELISABETH: Poor Adelheit, you didn't sleep all night; you needed your rest.—

ADELHEIT: If I only knew whether Hohenburg succeeded in convincing my husband of my innocence!

ELISABETH: I hope so, Adelheit. Listen, who's coming? (*Goes to the door.*) Look, it's Franz!

Scene 11

The preceding, Franz

FRANZ: Greetings, noble lady!

ADELHEIT: And to you, Franz. (*Looks at him sadly.*) Are you a messenger of peace or of misfortune?

FRANZ: Both.

ADELHEIT (*anxiously*): Make yourself understood, please!

FRANZ: Be calm, Mother—permit me to call you so—I wish to treat you honorably.

ADELHEIT: Then speak.

FRANZ (*sympathetically taking her hand*): Love and revenge are both pursuing you, are in fact preparing your grave; but you will not sink into that grave; I wish to save you.

ADELHEIT (*astounded*): You wish to save me—you?

FRANZ: Yes, I, the one whom you've never seemed to trust.

ADELHEIT: Forget that now, dear Franz, and tell me everything.

FRANZ: Are you ready?

ADELHEIT: I am.

FRANZ: My father returned from the contest, but he remained unconvinced of your innocence despite the knight's solemn oath to the contrary. "She must die," he said, and cold-bloodedly prepared to proclaim the death sentence on you himself. But you were

sleeping, so he ordered me to give you this poisonous powder.

> *During this speech Franz is visibly*
> *embarrassed, although Adelheit does not*
> *notice; Elisabeth is crying.*

ADELHEIT: And you accepted this order without protest?

FRANZ: At once, but only so that nobody else should receive it and prevent me from saving you.

ELISABETH: God, what a man!

ADELHEIT (*contemplatively*): Inconceivable! Up to now such
patience and consideration, and suddenly this ruth-
lessness. Robert, what awful change has taken place
in your heart!

FRANZ: Look, Mother (*pouring the powder out the window*),
away with death! (*Cheerfully.*) Now, make preparations to leave here with Elisabeth tonight at twelve.
You will find the doors unlocked, the tower guard
drugged, and the night watchman fled.

ADELHEIT: Suddenly you're so happy. One can see that
you are carrying out a good deed; heaven will
reward you for it.

FRANZ (*aside*): Not as good as you think. (*Aloud.*) I don't
deserve a reward.

ADELHEIT: But good Franz, I don't want to buy my freedom with your misfortune. What will your father
do to you when he learns of my escape?

FRANZ: Let that be my worry. The entire blame will fall on Curt, and he's gone. Take this ring Father gave me. You can get some money for it when you're in hiding.

ADELHEIT (*takes his hand*): This too! If I could only repay you, but I can do nothing except ask that you be blessed from above.

FRANZ (*upset*): Mother, Mother, your goodness, your misfortune—it's all overwhelming my heart. I can't stay in your presence any longer! May God be with you! (*Kisses her hand with extreme tenderness; quickly exits.*)

Scene 12

Adelheit, Elisabeth

ADELHEIT: May happiness and good fortune accompany you, noble youth, whom I so misjudged!— (*Weeps softly.*) Elisabeth, I'm not complaining. If I could look into the Almighty's ledger of sins, I might find that this terrible blow is not undeserved. Do you wish to remain faithful to me, dear girl, and follow your unfortunate friend wherever her furious fate drives her?

ELISABETH: Such is the call of both my duty and my heart. But shall we not seek refuge in Hohenburg's castle?

ADELHEIT: Oh, my dearest, I don't know what I should do. (*Thinking.*) It's true I should stay here, but unfortunately I'm no heroine who can easily face death. Let me rest a bit longer.

ACT 4

A grassy place with bushes. A section of the castle wall, at the end of which is a tower with a small door. Two small windows of the tower are dimly lit.

Scene 1

Hohenburg, Wenzel

Wenzel is disguised as a troubadour, with a harp or lute in his hand.

WENZEL (*looking all about*): The night watchman is no longer here. That's a good sign. You shall see, my lord, we've embarked on a successful venture.

HOHENBURG: I only hope that's what fate has in store for me! Look how sadly her lamp shines through those little windows. Poor prisoner! You have no idea that your Adelbert is waiting here beneath your cell, resolved to risk everything to save you.

WENZEL: Should we not take our places?

> *Hohenburg goes off toward the back of*
> *the tower.*

Scene 2

Wenzel

WENZEL (*seats himself near the door, plays, and sings*):
"The bravest of the knights of old
Once loved a maid so fair;
He went to war, another came,
With whom she soon was paired.
She sorrowed so both night and day,
They locked her up, just see!
The knight found out, returned at once,
His sweetheart to set free.
Thus love breaks through both bars and locks,
And even walls, it's said;
He took her on his noble steed,
And happily they fled."

Scene 3

Wenzel, Adelheit, Elisabeth

The door opens, and Adelheit and Elisabeth
emerge cautiously.

WENZEL: Perfect! Here they come, by themelves. (*Pulls his hat down over his eyes.*) I have to disguise myself a bit.

ADELHEIT (*quietly*): Who was that singing just now?

WENZEL (*altering his voice*): Just a poor troubadour.

ADELHEIT: I trust you are an honorable man.

WENZEL: I hope so.

ADELHEIT: Will you accompany us for a ways if we pay you?

WENZEL: To wherever you wish, but wait a moment, I have a friend nearby whom I must call first.

ELISABETH: Can we trust him, too?

WENZEL: As well as me. Listen, noble ladies, you couldn't fall into better hands than ours; we've come here together to free you. (*Pushes back his hat and assumes his natural voice again.*) The knight Adelbert is also not far away.

ADELHEIT and ELISABETH (*together*): Oh, Wenzel!—

WENZEL: You see, I'm always at your command.

Scene 4

The preceding, Hohenburg

HOHENBURG: What stroke of good fortune brings us together again so soon?

WENZEL: I think I pulled off an Orpheus trick; the door just opened at my song.

HOHENBURG: Quiet, this is no time for joking! (*To Adelheit.*) I came here to free you from your prison cell by treachery or by force, and I find that you have escaped by yourself.— Explain this puzzle to me.

ADELHEIT: Rastenberg ordered Franz to poison me in his absence.

HOHENBURG: Oh how vile! I thought I had convinced him of your innocence.

ADELHEIT: It seems he only pretended to be convinced. Trustworthy Franz revealed everything to me and arranged for my escape.

HOHENBURG: Thank God, my dear lady! Now won't you accompany me with a willing heart?

ADELHEIT (*fearfully giving him her hand*): Since fate itself has chosen you to be my leader, it can no longer be a crime to follow you.

HOHENBURG: Hurry, Wenzel, bring the horses. (*Wenzel exits.*) Come, my love.

Scene 5

Adelheit, Hohenburg, Elisabeth

ADELHEIT (*takes a few steps but then suddenly stops*): Oh Hohenburg, suddenly I'm overcome with fear; I cannot leave. Allow me to stay here until your men come.

HOHENBURG (*helps her to a boulder by the bushes*): Adelheit! You're trembling even though you are under my protection.—

ADELHEIT: I think I hear something.

HOHENBURG: Don't be afraid; it's just the wind in the trees.

ADELHEIT: Look around to make sure everything is safe; I am more and more frightened.

HOHENBURG: I already checked everywhere and didn't see or hear anything. (*Listening.*) And it is still quiet.

ADELHEIT: I beg you to look around; you too, Elisabeth.

HOHENBURG: If it makes you feel better—

> *Hohenburg goes off in one direction,*
> *Elisabeth in another. Meanwhile Bertha,*
> *disguised in a cloak, comes up behind*
> *Adelheit, plunges a dagger into her*
> *breast, then disappears again.*

ADELHEIT (*slipping from the boulder*): Help! Help! Murder!

HOHENBURG: God! What is this?

ELISABETH: What misfortune!

HOHENBURG (*lifts Adelheit onto the boulder again; she sinks against his breast; Elisabeth kneels next to her*): You are bleeding!— (*Pressing the wound.*) God in heaven! Where did this blow come from?

ELISABETH: May the saints take pity on you!

ADELHEIT (*weakly*): I don't know. But I think that we have all been deceived and that Robert—is innocent. Be reconciled with him, dear Adelbert, and tell him that this bleeding heart did suffer because it had no love— for him.— Will you?

HOHENBURG: You dear, unfortunate one! I will do everything you wish. (*In pain.*) If only the heavens would
allow you to live.

Scene 6

The preceding, Wenzel

WENZEL (*arriving out of breath*): Knight, we are all waiting
over there; what's taking you so long? (*Startled.*)
What has happened?

ELISABETH: Murder, abominable murder!

HOHENBURG (*to Wenzel*): Go for help!

Wenzel starts to go.

ADELHEIT (*weaker*): Stay—I bid you—it found its mark—
all too well. (*To Hohenburg.*) We believed that we
were destined for one another, but—didn't I say it
yesterday!—in that other world.— (*Folds her hands,
gazes toward heaven, and dies; Elisabeth secretly speaks
to Wenzel.*)

HOHENBURG (*extremely moved*): Adelheit! Adelheit! Awaken
but once more! Awaken! (*Kisses her; listens for her
breathing.*) In vain!— This noble spirit has flown.

ELISABETH (*crying loudly*): Oh my beloved, unfortunate
friend!

HOHENBURG: She is no longer unfortunate; she has found heavenly peace—but me—pity me!

WENZEL: Good sir, how your suffering moves me.

HOHENBURG (*placing Adelheit in Elisabeth's arms*): Sleep peacefully, dearest martyr of the most tender love. In life you were stolen away from me; in death nothing shall tear you from me! (*To Wenzel and Elisabeth.*) Let her rest in my chapel; I will kneel before the Almighty on her gravestone and pray for comfort. Come, Wenzel!

WENZEL: Where to, my stern lord?

HOHENBURG: To do our duty: to find the murderer.

Scene 7

The preceding, Bertha

BERTHA (*furiously stepping out from behind the bushes; throwing off her cloak*): My revenge would not be half as sweet if I didn't tell you this myself: Bertha von Wildenau murdered your beloved!

HOHENBURG (*pulls his sword*): Impudent fool! Take your punishment.

BERTHA (*retreating*): Too late, too late; death already gnaws at me. I took poison.

WENZEL: Horrible creature!

HOHENBURG: Then go to hell, sinner, and receive the just reward there for your black deeds.

ELISABETH: Unnatural, despicable woman!

HOHENBURG: What did this innocent soul do, to make you murder her?

BERTHA: Much, very much! She blocked my way to your heart. From the enormity of my revenge, judge the enormity of my former love for you.

HOHENBURG: Monster! (*Gnashes his teeth.*) Oh, that you hadn't preceded me with your suicide!

BERTHA (*with mocking laughter*): Ha! (*Points to Adelheit.*) Someone who can take revenge in this manner easily has the courage to kill herself.

WENZEL: She's mad.

BERTHA: Don't be so sure, boy; (*pointing to her forehead*) here it may be burning hot; but—I know what I did.

Scene 8

The preceding, Franz

FRANZ (*aghast*): What dreadful deeds! (*Approaches Bertha.*) Bertha, my Bertha!

BERTHA (*shoving him away*): Knave! You're released from your oath to avenge me; see what I was able to accomplish alone.

HOHENBURG (*with revulsion*): Do not sully yourself with her; she has murdered Adelheit and taken poison.

FRANZ (*shuddering*): You miserable creature, what have you done?

Hohenburg walks over to Adelheit's body and kisses her.

BERTHA: Thanks to you and your cowardice, I've become a double murderer!—

FRANZ: Not cowardice—it was human kindness that kept me from carrying out your charge. But you were supposed to think that Adelheit had escaped before I could get to her. How did you find out?

BERTHA: From your faithful friend, Curt, who's long been my secret informer.

FRANZ (*furious*): That traitor!—

WENZEL: Countess, you are about to meet your stern Judge. Don't you wish to seek His forgiveness?

FRANZ (*with compassion*): Yes, Bertha, I beg you.

BERTHA: Silence, cowards!

HOHENBURG: Begone, miserable creature! You are not worthy of dying where Adelheit died.

BERTHA: I don't intend to. But let me feast my eyes once more on the sight of your beloved, for whom you rejected me so proudly. (*Looks at Adelheit.*) Look at her lying there, so bloody, so maimed!

WENZEL: Get back, demon.

Hohenburg angrily pulls his sword again and
threatens her.

BERTHA: Have you forgotten that I took the poison? Will you compete with death? Look, here come my people.

Scene 9

The preceding, Bertha's entourage,
carrying torches

CHAMBERMAID: For heaven's sake, Countess, what are you doing here? We missed you at such a late hour, so we hurried to find you.

BERTHA: I had to take care of a matter for which I didn't need your help.

HOHENBURG (*to Bertha's servants*): I beg you, remove this murderer from my sight.

CHAMBERMAID: Murderer?— Ah, she was so distraught all evening long; we were afraid something awful was going to happen.

BERTHA (*in convulsions*): Oh, oh! Get me away before death overtakes me here. (*Wildly looking around.*) How dark everything grows before my eyes! It is the night of eternal damnation! (*With a hideous shudder.*) I'm coming—I'm coming—!

CHAMBERMAID: May heaven have mercy on her. We are innocent of these evil deeds.

Bertha is carried off.

Scene 10

Franz, Hohenburg

FRANZ: Noble, courageous knight, take pity on me. I fell into her lascivious net; but at least I was not meant to die in it. (*Sinks to his knees beside Adelheit's body and kisses her hand.*) You good, devout, long-suffering soul, forgive me.

HOHENBURG: Franz, I am at a loss to explain all these horrible events. Follow me to my castle, where we can take the full measure of our sorrow together.

FRANZ: I am happy to follow you, Knight. I cannot stay in our castle. Oh my father, my wronged father; he'll never forgive me.

HOHENBURG (*composing himself*): He must. At first light I shall send Wenzel to him. In the meantime, let us arrange to have these precious remains borne away.

ACT 5

A chamber in Hohenburg's castle.

Scene 1

Hohenburg

HOHENBURG (*alone, sitting deep in thought, with his hand on his heart*): How my heart has changed! There's nothing left of the passion that sought to crush every obstacle, sweep away all in its path. (*Pauses.*) The deceptive gleam of my heated imagination fades, and before my eyes everything takes on the color of truth. The way fate seemed to lead me through so many dangers back to this place, the way Adelheit seemed still to harbor love for me, and the way circumstances seemed to support my plans—all that blinded me and led me to believe that heaven itself looked favorably upon my misguided passion. But fate was only testing me, and I ought to have stood up to that test like a man, but I—failed it! Adelheit,

Adelheit, you were stronger, wiser than I. I should have listened to your gentle warnings and locked up my love in the sanctum of my heart; I should have treated Bertha less severely, so that she would never have resorted to this horrible act of revenge!— Almighty God, You have forgiven me so often; forgive me once more, and I shall return to the banner of the Cross and wash away my weakness in the blood of the enemies of Your faith!—

Scene 2

Hohenburg, Franz

HOHENBURG: Did you rest, Franz?

FRANZ: One as miserable as I does not rest. His is a bed of thorns, and tears are his sleeping potion.

HOHENBURG: Poor Franz! At least try to look composed; your father will soon be here.

FRANZ: Oh my father!

HOHENBURG: You have nothing to fear. We are both guiltier than you. You were seduced, but—we—

Scene 3

The preceding, one of Hohenburg's servants; then Rastenberg with his followers

SERVANT: The knight Robert is entering the castle with his entourage. (*Exits.*)

HOHENBURG: He's returning sooner than I thought. Franz, look how misfortune can change our mood. I shall never again see in him the hated rival, the very sight of whom caused my blood to boil.— He has become my companion on this road of sorrow. Because he also embodies what little remains of my lost beloved, my heart is drawn to him.

RASTENBERG (*enters with his followers and Wenzel*): Good day to you, Sir Knight!

HOHENBURG: Welcome under the roof of a friend. Has our shared sorrowful fate also made you my friend?

RASTENBERG: Hohenburg, it is no longer an uncontrollable, spiteful man you see before you.— Sorrow has humbled me.

HOHENBURG: Oh, what a profound effect it has on the human heart! I am no longer the man I was either.

RASTENBERG (*to his squires*): Remove my armor. I am done fighting.

They remove his armor.

HOHENBURG: Then you forgive me for trying to steal Adelheit from you, for leading her to her death with my unbridled passion?

RASTENBERG: Do you forgive me for stealing her from you in the first place?

HOHENBURG: With all my heart.

RASTENBERG: Then we are reconciled for good.

65

HOHENBURG (*leading Franz up to him*): And now forgive your son.

RASTENBERG: You are here, too, Franz? So this house has become a gathering place for anguished souls.

FRANZ: Oh father, don't close your heart to my misery.

RASTENBERG (*extremely moved*): Come here, my son, let me press you to my ravaged heart; pity me as I pity you. Let my example and your brief, sad experience with Bertha teach you to flee the seductive pleasures of love and lust. Their chalices brim with sweet liquor, but poison lies at the bottom. (*Embraces him tightly.*) I never thought that sorrow and lamentation would accompany our reunion.

FRANZ: My dear, tormented father, do you forgive me?

RASTENBERG: If I were not to forgive you, a victim of temptation, how could God ever forgive me? Oh, I am the most guilty of us all! But I have decided to seek atonement in the strictest monastic order.

HOHENBURG: What do I hear, Rastenberg? Your bravery can still benefit the world; you have many duties yet to perform.

RASTENBERG: The world has seen my bravery and my weakness; any duties left undone I entrust to Franz's heart and hope he will fulfill them with honor, for these youthful events will instill manliness in him.

FRANZ (*in a solemn tone*): I swear in the name of all the holy saints that your faith in me will not be disappointed. You do still intend to give me your noble name?

RASTENBERG: That will be my last worldly deed. Now, Hohenburg, embrace your friend.

The knights embrace.

HOHENBURG: Adelheit's spirit hovers about this embrace and blesses us.

RASTENBERG: Tell me, did she mention me in her last moments? Wenzel reported everything to me, but this he didn't know.

HOHENBURG: Certainly she thought of you; it still pained her bleeding heart that she had not been able to return your love.

RASTENBERG: What a noble woman! I often observed her inner turmoil. But now she is victorious. (*To his squires.*) Accept my thanks for your faithfulness and your service; thanks to you, too, Wenzel, for coming to me as a friend. I will remember all of you before I depart this earth.

The squires exit.

Scene 4

The preceding, Hermit

HERMIT: Peace be with you.

FRANZ: In all eternity!

HOHENBURG: Have you come to comfort us, benevolent friend? Oh, if only I had taken your reverent warnings, your predictions about my undertaking, more to heart! Now the time has come that I repent, only too late.

HERMIT: Repentance is the best, the most pleasing sacrifice. God views it with grace and heals the tormented heart of the penitent. (*Shyly.*) Noble knights, may I not speak with the two of you alone for a little while?

> *Hohenburg gestures to Franz, who exits*
> *sighing loudly, while the hermit observes*
> *Franz closely.*

Scene 5

Rastenberg, Hohenburg, Hermit

RASTENBERG (*to the hermit*): The sound of your voice stirred me yesterday, and today it awakens a memory in my soul that intensifies my suffering. Tell me—

HERMIT (*interrupting him*): May this trembling voice move you as intensely as it awakens your memory. Oh, I cannot, I cannot maintain this deception any longer! (*Tears off beard and hood; her hair falls to her shoulders and she to Rastenberg's feet.*) Forgive me, Rastenberg, forgive me!

RASTENBERG: Am I to suffer this blow, too? Franziska! You unfortunate creature; you were banished by me. How is it that you are here?

HOHENBURG: What a sight!

RASTENBERG: Behold here in the guise of a hermit the unfaithful woman I once rejected, (*moved*) Franz's mother.

HOHENBURG: Incredible!

RASTENBERG: Speak, woman, how did you come to assume this disguise?

FRANZISKA: Forgive me, Rastenberg, forgive me!

RASTENBERG (*lifting her up*): Well, I can forgive (*with increasing emotion*) the raging pain that pierced my breast—the burning tears that clouded my manly eyes—the lamentation of my son—all these consequences of your betrayal I can forgive. (*Turning away his face.*) I wish I could forgive your black infidelity as well.

FRANZISKA: If you can't forget, heartless man, that I was the victim of a seduction, then also don't forget that

69

I was your first and warmest love, that I risked my life to give you your one and only son, that I was ready to follow you to a grave in the Holy Land despite the many pitfalls that threaten the weaker sex, but that I was forced to remain behind without protection in a foreign land. Are you listening, Knight— don't forget this, don't forget this either!

HOHENBURG: Robert, no good deed deserves to go unfulfilled. Let the memory of that awful event be erased in your memory. See in Franziska only a repentant woman who has been guided here by heaven itself to achieve a reconciliation.

RASTENBERG: Franziska!— This will be the last time I remind you of your guilt. As the mother of my son, embrace me!

FRANZISKA: What joy! Now I shall gladly depart this earth.

RASTENBERG: Live, unfortunate woman, so that you may find the peace that I have lost.

FRANZISKA: Oh, I can feel how this meeting has been too strong for my tired spirit, for my ravaged body—I shall not survive for long, but again, now I die gladly, for I have seen my Robert once more. With God I have long since been reconciled by way of sincere repentance and severe atonement, but not with you. This awareness tortured me mercilessly. My veil, saturated with tears, and my countless sighs echoing in the narrow cloisters of the convent aroused the pity of one of the nuns; I confided to her my grief about you, my longing for you, and she helped me escape. I arrived unnoticed in this region and found the hermitage and the hermit, who was in his last throes. He gave up the ghost as I prayed for him; I buried him, put on his robe, and have been living in blessed solitude since then. Your Adelheit came to see me with Elisabeth. Her appearance touched me; I gained her trust; she told me of her fate and then returned to see me on that sorrowful day to seek solace from me, from me, who was desperately in need of solace herself! In the meantime I was blessed with frequent news about you and our son, and I eagerly waited to catch sight of both of you. The day before yesterday, treachery led you to my hut, but I didn't dare reveal myself to you in the state you were in; I could only affirm Adelheit's innocence. (*Touchingly.*) Robert, now that this Adelheit has been wrested from you, allow me to mourn her beside you, to take care of you, and to conclude the short remainder of my sad life in your castle.

RASTENBERG (*sympathetically*): Franziska! I am not able to comply with your request. I have renounced the world.

FRANZISKA (*sinking into a chair*): You have?— Where did I find this one last weak ray of worldly hope? (*Glancing toward the heavens.*) Upward, O heart, that's where your happiness beckons.

HOHENBURG: Take courage, good woman; happiness still awaits you here. I will bring your son to your arms.

FRANZISKA: (*as if waking from a dream*): My son—my son!— Can he have been the one who left us earlier?

HOHENBURG: The very same.

FRANZISKA: My heart started pounding when I saw the youth before, but in my state of misery I did not understand what it meant. Go, brave knight, bring him the message that his mother is waiting here and is gathering her last strength to give him a kiss of greeting and of parting. And yet, will he acknowledge me as his mother and not despise me?

HOHENBURG: Have no fear. Only a villain can tear asunder the bonds of nature. (*Exits.*)

Scene 6

Franziska, Rastenberg

FRANZISKA (*trustingly*): How are you, Robert?

RASTENBERG: I am in great pain. How could it be otherwise? (*Gesturing toward his breast.*) Heavy burdens crush me here.

FRANZISKA: Yet you do not collapse! Yes, the Creator gave your sex the advantage in strength to endure. I feel how I am a mere woman. Your arm, good Robert—I am fainting—

RASTENBERG (*supporting her*): Compose yourself; I hear Franz coming.

FRANZISKA: Franz—this name gives me strength.

Scene 7

The preceding, Franz, Hohenburg

HOHENBURG: This is your repentant, gentle mother.

FRANZISKA (*rushes into Franz's arms*): Oh, my son!

FRANZ (*with the strongest feeling*): Mother, Mother! All my feelings are contained in this word.

RASTENBERG: Regard her with reverence; she is reconciled both with God and with your father.

FRANZ (*pressing her to his breast*): I have no words.

FRANZISKA (*weak*): My boy! Your life began beneath my heart—and now mine will end next to yours.—(*Weaker.*) Farewell! May God bless—all of you.

FRANZ (*in extreme sorrow*): God! She is dying.

RASTENBERG: May her soul rest in peace! My strength is ebbing as well. Hohenburg, I present to you my son.

HOHENBURG: Let us flee from this place, Franz, from this scene of despair. Do you wish to follow me on a new Crusade to the Holy Land?

FRANZ (*gently lays the body of his mother down and kisses her*): The sooner the better, Knight, the sooner the better. I yearn for the sound of battle.

RASTENBERG (*to Hohenburg*): Be a father to him, teach him to fight; I shall pray for you at the foot of the altar.

HOHENBURG: We will do battle and conquer, or else die with honor.

FRANZ (*with enthusiasm*): I wish to die for my faith. (*Bends over the body of his mother.*) Let this tear be the last offering of my tenderness.

RASTENBERG (*taking Franziska's hand*): Sleep, good friend of my youth, sleep until that grand day when the Creator will take mercy on us all. Hohenburg! Allow me now to visit Adelheit's grave.

HOHENBURG (*extending his hand*): Come, I will accompany you to that consecrated place.

Curtain.